margie m

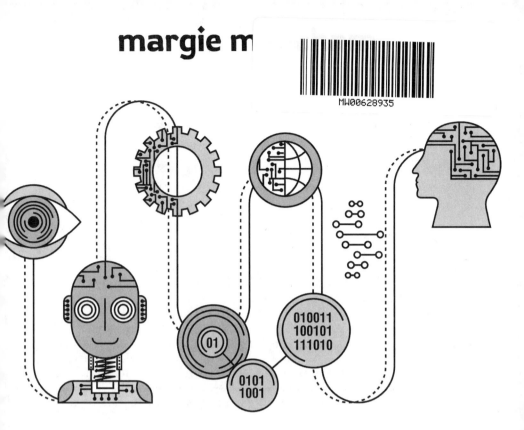

ai in talent development

development

capitalize on the ai revolution to transform
the way you work, learn, and live

PRESS

ATD Press is an internationally renowned source of insightful and practical information on talent development, training, and professional development.

ATD Press
1640 King Street
Alexandria, VA 22314 USA

Ordering information: Books published by ATD Press can be purchased by visiting ATD's website at td.org/books or by calling 800.628.2783 or 703.683.8100.

Library of Congress Control Number: 2020946220

ISBN-10: 1-95049-631-7
ISBN-13: 978-1-95049-631-0
e-ISBN: 978-1-95049-632-7

ATD Press Editorial Staff
Director: Sarah Halgas
Manager: Melissa Jones
Content Manager, Science of Learning: Alexandria Clapp
Developmental Editor: Jack Harlow
Production Editor: Hannah Sternberg
Copy Editor: Caroline Coppel
Text Design: Shirley E.M. Raybuck
Cover Design: Shirley E.M. Raybuck

Printed by Data Reproductions Corporation, Auburn Hills, MI

Contents

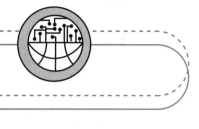

Tips on How to Use This Book

How many books have you bought lately?

I realize that no matter how many books you buy, the decision represents an investment of your money and time, and I take your decision to buy *AI in Talent Development* seriously. So, I'd like to ask you to think about how many nonfiction books you've purchased over the years. Play with me for a moment and write down a number. (It's OK if this is a wildly imprecise guess; it's just a starting point for building your plan to get the most benefit from this book.) Now, how many of those books have you actually finished? Write that number down. Finally, of those books, how many practical ideas do you think you implemented as a direct result of reading them? I imagine that you're very busy, that the demands of your profession and the limited amount of resources available force you to make hard choices about how you spend your time. Because your time is precious to me—and I want this book to make the final list of books that you have **read and used**—I'm offering a few suggestions for maximizing your time and getting the most tangible benefits possible from your reading experience.

Tell Someone You Are Reading This Book

Why do organizations like Alcoholics Anonymous encourage their members to share their plans and challenges with other members? It's because they understand the power of social commitments to keep us on track. If you want to finish any project, one of the best ways to achieve that goal is to tell everyone you know what you're doing. Today's social media environment gives you a chance to let everyone in your circle witness your excitement and commitment. It's not just a nice "photo op" for your Facebook page; it's an effective tool for stimulating creative ideas and putting those ideas into practice.

Take Notes by Hand

The note-taking process has a powerful effect on the learning process. While you are reading, you'll form questions, ideas, and plans to apply what you read to your situation. These tenuous thoughts are the beginnings of true learning, the start of new neural pathways that you must nurture if you intend to get the greatest benefit possible from this book. If you already keep a journal, you know the power of this habit to focus your thoughts and shape your choices in life. If you've been thinking about keeping a journal, or you've fallen off the habit and would like to reboot this powerful practice, let this book be an opportunity to begin.

Review the Table of Contents as a Preview

No doubt you will feel more interested in some topics than others. Take note of those feelings—that's your brain beginning to link your prior experience to the new experience of reading this book. It's also a great place to start writing. Just capture questions, ideas, and other thoughts that flash into your mind as you review the titles of the chapters.

Pick a Place That Interests You and Start Reading

Some of you will want to start with chapter 1 and continue in linear fashion. (This is how I personally like to read an informational book, but that doesn't mean it's the right approach for you.) Start with the chapters that seem most interesting to you. If you feel the need to go back to an earlier chapter to pick up some background information, you can always do so later.

Avoid Skimming

But here's the challenge: Just because you're turning the pages doesn't mean you are actually reading. You may be skimming. Skimming is a technique for skipping over letters, words, and even sentences and paragraphs to gain a general sense of reading material. It used to be taught in grade school as a first step toward reading a textbook or research paper, to prepare you to get as much out of the content as possible. When you skim something, your brain connects information you already know with information you see on the page.

It is an excellent method for preparing you to understand and integrate new information. Unfortunately, many of us have learned to get by with skimming a webpage, an email, or a report and never quite get to the reading part.

Viewing text on screens tends to encourage us to skim, rather than take the time to actually read and think about what we're reading. This behavior is becoming so common that college professors and employers are concerned that people may not even know how to read for deeper understanding anymore (Wolf 2018).

Access the Glossary Whenever You Encounter an Unfamiliar Term

While most of the terms used in this book have become fairly common knowledge, you may sometimes be surprised by the difference between the definition as you "know it" and the one you find discussed in this book. Don't be too concerned about these differences. In researching this book, I found that many experts disagree on the definitions. In the interest of consistency, I've standardized my definitions using the "Machine Learning Glossary" published online by Google. No doubt there are many other sources available, but this one is frequently cited by artificial intelligence (AI) developers, so I'm comfortable sharing it with you.

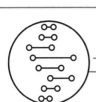

Introduction

The angel of death. Beautiful, isn't it? A perfect sphere radiating from some kind of inner light, punctuated by trumpet-shaped protrusions that might be arms, sensor probes, ornaments, or even the eyes of a strange new insect or alien being. Is it a disco ball discovered in your granny's basement, an exotic planet in a distant galaxy, or an artificial neuron whipped up in a lab? It could be a Christmas ornament, or even a Christmas angel, sparkling with the message of hope and dazzling in its brilliance.

But it's none of these things. It's the well-known image of the novel coronavirus.

As I write this, the world is deep into the pandemic of 2019–2020, fighting a new and highly contagious virus that delivers the multispectrum disease we call COVID-19. Although many people who contract the virus suffer only mild symptoms, others become violently ill, and sadly, some of those people die. In the absence of a cure, a vaccine, or even reliable treatments, our only weapon at the moment is behavior change. We are teaching people to follow sanitation and containment protocols that are clumsy and inconvenient. We're changing the way we work and buy simple things, like groceries and fast food. Schools closed almost overnight, leaving much of the burden of keeping their kids entertained and educated on the shoulders of parents, who were adjusting to working from home and learning how to homeschool their children at the same time. Traditional "brick and mortar" colleges and universities quickly converted to online education. Airline travel, restaurants, grocery stores, department stores, movie theaters, swimming pools, rock concerts, shopping malls—all part of our modern experience—have been shut down or severely curtailed.

This crisis is making many of us rethink our priorities as we draw the circles of our lives ever inward, making our physical world as small as possible in the hope of keeping ourselves and our loved ones safe. At the same time, Internet usage has exploded, as we turn outward to a digital world to educate and entertain ourselves, staying connected with friends and family we can no longer reach out and touch in the physical world, at least for now.

The scope and urgency of this crisis is putting the learning profession in the spotlight. This isn't the first time we've been asked to respond to a global crisis, and it certainly won't be the last. The most recent event prior to the current pandemic started before I was born and lasted through my childhood.

The Race for Space: A Lesson in Magnificent Desolation

In 1957, the Soviet Union successfully launched the first man-made satellite into orbit around Earth, creating what was believed to be an existential crisis in the "free world." The United States and other countries in the West perceived this achievement by a communist nation as an imminent threat. If we were unable to answer this threat, the logic went, we might one day be wiped out by weapons from space. A crisis is an excellent mechanism for focusing public attention and gaining federal funding to solve a problem.

In 1961, when President John F. Kennedy said, "We choose to go to the moon," many people thought he was crazy. From a strictly logical perspective, we had absolutely no business putting three human beings in a tin can, strapping them onto a partially controlled bomb, and launching them into the seemingly endless and deadly abyss of space, 239,000 miles from home. Maybe it was the inspiring vision of a dynamic and persuasive leader, maybe it was the general paranoia brought on by the Cold War with Russia, or maybe it was just our natural human arrogance, but something inside our collective consciousness said, "Why not? Let's go for it."

Eight years, $49.4 billion (that's $490 billion in today's dollars), and three lost lives later, Neil Armstrong and Buzz Aldrin became the first humans to step onto the moon, while Michael Collins kept the lights burning on the Command and Service Module.

As he bounced along the surface, Aldrin described the lunar landscape as "beautiful, beautiful, magnificent desolation." Magnificent, as he pondered the sheer power of the engineering feat and the labor of more than 100,000 people to land him on this cold rock. Desolate because there was no sign of life as far as he could see.

Kennedy had set the goal of completing this mission by the end of the decade. Perhaps the most remarkable fact of this achievement is that they also came back safely, four days later. During the "race to the moon," education was highly valued in Western society. Americans invested in schools and emphasized courses in science and math. Discoveries that helped us land on the moon also gave us major advances in medicine, telecommunications, information technology, electronics, navigation, medicine, food preservation, and many other practical fields. The number-one goal of nearly every kid was to grow up to become an astronaut.

At the time, most people expected the moon landing to be the first of many advances in science and technology to follow, all led by the United States, the recognized leader in science, technology, healthcare, and overall standard of living at the time. But the moon shot didn't belong just to the people of the United States. It was watched live all over the world, and inspired many to envision a new era of prosperity and hope, all powered by the advancement of education and science.

But it didn't happen quite that way. Sadly, we have been living in a period of magnificent desolation for some time now. In an era of unprecedented technology, the human race is more ignorant of science than ever. Many college students are less capable of putting together a coherent sentence than their less-educated parents, and many people believe that science is something you can choose to "believe in" or not.

That is why I wrote this book.

Today, nearly every scientist in the world has turned to focus on conquering the coronavirus. One of the most important tools we have in a race against the angel of death is artificial intelligence (AI). As a matter of fact, the Blue Dot algorithm first alerted the world to a new and potentially deadly virus that had "jumped" from animals to humans. The Blue Dot algorithm searches airline travel and news reports to uncover emerging trends that signal the spread of related diseases (Niiler 2020). So AI was part of the story from the beginning.

As it became clear that this was no ordinary virus, but a dangerous pandemic, neuroscientists who had been using machine learning to map the complexities of the human brain began using it to sift through oceans of data to find a cure or a vaccine. Recognizing patterns, confirming or disproving hypotheses, predicting trends, and poring over decades of research are all tasks that machine learning is well suited to perform—and AI can do it faster and much more accurately than an army of humans. Although it is my fervent hope that these smart people and their algorithms will help us find a way out of the current health crisis, it is also very likely that we will make major discoveries that have immediate, practical applications in other fields along the way. The same programs that are analyzing medical data today might be identifying training gaps in a major organization tomorrow. The young people who are choosing careers in AI to fight the virus will remain in their profession once the imminent danger has passed, and they will be smarter and more confident in their ability to apply AI to solve the biggest problems of their world.

In this book, we'll talk about how AI is transforming the way we learn, such as personalizing learning experiences based on individual student interests and progress, assessing organizational needs based on financial forecasts, and even delivering education directly to students in the place of a teacher. These applications exist today, and they can only be accelerated by the work being done on COVID-19. Eventually, we will find the solution to COVID-19, and when that happens, we all will know a lot more about artificial intelligence, big data, and the power of science.

I believe that the learning profession—the teachers, trainers, and educators of the world—has taken a central position during the pandemic that will continue long after the initial danger has subsided. It will be up to us to continue to demonstrate our value. We can do this by being on the leading edge of emergent technology, rather than by simply following and reacting to requests from our stakeholders. One of our most compelling opportunities to lead will be in the implementation of artificial intelligence, which is getting a huge boost of attention and investment in response to the desperate need for answers that we humans are painfully slow in developing on our own.

I am absolutely certain that we will all be changed by the experience of surviving the pandemic. Despite our whimsical and understandable desire to turn back the clock, there will be no "going back to normal." Once the initial threat has passed, there will be a new normal that has actually been creeping up on us for a long time.

As with any revolution, the AI transformation didn't just happen overnight. Back in 2016, just a few short years and a lifetime ago, I was one of the first learning-science writers to point out that the fields of neuroscience and AI were converging. I wasn't looking for it. I was happily running my consulting business, helping schools and corporate training departments apply cognitive science, when I wrote a blog post about intelligence. The more I researched the neuroscience evidence for a new understanding of human intelligence, the more I kept bumping into discoveries and models based on artificial intelligence. I posited that it was impossible to talk about one without the other, and noted that the two disciplines were engaged in a virtuous cycle that was propelling both disciplines forward, leveraging advances from each other to make great leaps in understanding all kinds of intelligence—whether carbon or silicon based. At the time, I was surprised and encouraged by the response from neuroscientists and psychology professors. I knew that thousands of trainers, training managers, and university professors read my blog, but I never thought to get the attention of the scientific community.

I realized that I was onto something important; it had become impossible to be an expert in adult learning without also being an expert in machine learning. That insight has changed how I view myself, my clients, and the work I've been called to do.

My Story, My Calling

My good friend John was the best man at my wedding, more than 30 years ago. After completing his education and becoming a certified pharmacist, he went back to school to become an MD. As every doctor will probably tell you, advising your friends and family on matters of health goes with the territory. One day I was apologizing to John for taking up his time with a question like this when he said something powerful to me: "Margie, don't ever apologize for asking me to be a doctor. This is what I do. This is my calling."

It's funny how we arrive at our calling in life, isn't it? When I met John we were both still in school, and he already "knew" he wanted to be a pharmacist. He changed his path when he found his calling, his own personal way to bring value to the world. While some may have a clear sense of mission from an early age, I just wanted to get a job out of college. I was already married, and income was a pressing need. While I was still in school, I was trying out for a secretarial pool job when a recruiter heard my fingers flying over the keyboard during my typing test and rushed me across town to be trained to work on a word processor. Within a month I was working extra hours performing backups on huge floppy disks and automating little processes to make the work more efficient. After college, I took a job in sales for the summer, fully expecting to teach highschool English in the fall. I soon discovered that all those slick "techniques" my trainer taught me weren't nearly as useful as my psychology and education classes. I simply sat down and started teaching my customers how the product would change their lives. After being the top salesperson in the region for five years in a row, I was invited to start a sales training program. At the time, it never occurred to me that I was putting my education training into practice. It was just a nice, new job. And when I took advantage of the company tuition assistance program to earn a master's degree in adult education technology, I never thought I'd be writing about neuroscience and artificial intelligence 10 years later.

When I left my corporate training leader job to start my own consulting business, I didn't realize that the same people who were my bosses would soon be hiring me as their newly minted learning consultant. And then, a few years into a successful consulting career, I wrote that blog post about intelligence. Then someone invited me to speak at a training conference, and another and another. After I wrote a book, more speaking opportunities followed. I designed a course, "Essentials of Brain-Based Learning," for ATD and started talking about the AI-neuroscience connection in my webinars. One day, I was talking to a friend at ATD about an idea for a book, and he encouraged me to pursue it.

Today I'm showing companies how to use chatbots to deliver learning content and assess knowledge, how to deploy AI to build truly personalized coaching tools, and how to design any learning experience with the brain in mind, using models that come directly from machine learning experiments.

It may seem that I was just bouncing from job to job, and it certainly felt that way sometimes. But now I look back and see that I wasn't taking random sideways steps; I was following a path—my path. A meandering, leisurely journey toward my realization that I have something unique to offer, and that gift is wrapped up in my ability to translate the complexities of science into practical changes we can make today to improve the way we live, love, and learn.

And then I wrote this book.

About This Book

AI in Talent Development was written for you—human resource managers, trainers, instructional designers, and talent development professionals—to share what I know about the benefits, uses, and risks of artificial intelligence technology in our field. I describe specific actions that can be implemented now to take advantage of innovations in AI-powered talent development and help prepare you and your organization for the evolving AI revolution.

Here is a description of the chapters.

Chapter 1: Wake Up and Smell the Coffee

In this chapter, I share some everyday applications of AI that you may not have even noticed, yet they are all around you. We'll explore a brief history of man's endeavors to build a digital version of himself and clarify a few terms that I will use throughout the book.

Chapter 2: Reboot Yourself With a Robot

One of the most practical advantages of deploying AI is how it can make us all more productive, by automating repetitive tasks, streamlining processes, and helping us keep track of our busy days. Rebooting yourself might sound a bit frightening, but this chapter is really about simple, fun, and practical ways to ease into AI that will yield big benefits for very little effort.

Chapter 3: Have a Chat With a Machine

One of the most immediate use cases for the learning profession is deploying chatbots to help people learn. The applications range from using intelligent bots as simple user interfaces to deploying engaging, "lifelike" coaches and role-play partners.

Chapter 4: Make Your Learning Management System Smarter

For decades, the holy grail of education has been to deliver truly customized learning experiences, education, and training that are shaped by the needs of each individual. The irony of the explosion of big data is that the more we know about all the learners in our system, the more we can discover about each individual, and the more effectively we'll be able to tailor our content to what each person needs, just when they need it.

Chapter 5: Do the Right Thing

This chapter is about the ethical considerations of deploying AI. Along with its many benefits, every new technology creates new risks, forcing us to recognize our responsibility to take care in how we deploy that technology. In the case of artificial intelligence, it can be hard to tell right from wrong, because so much is still unknown, and the consequences of our decisions don't always appear until some time has passed. However, with great risk comes great reward. I believe that teachers, trainers, and others who are drawn to the learning profession have a responsibility to lead in this regard. We'll talk about a few practical ways to do that in this chapter.

Chapter 6: Where Do We Go From Here?

As your guide through this book, I have a responsibility too. I can't just dump a lot of information on you and tell you to go out there and make things happen. I promise in this last chapter to do my best to pull this all together and perhaps show you your own meandering path toward who you are becoming.

Appendix

In this section you will find an annotated list of recommended online and print resources, and fillable and printable templates, planners, and tools. There are also several ways to help you stay in touch. You'll find links to my blog, podcast, social media accounts, and online courses. On my website, learningtogo.info, you'll find links to all these resources, as well as a schedule of my speaking appearances, publications, and workshops.

Resource Page

Because the fields of AI and learning technology are so fluid, I've included a separate resource page online. This page will give you access to additional tools mentioned in the book, such as worksheets, reading lists, and templates. You'll also have a chance to join in an ongoing discussion about the use of AI to advance learning.

Contact Me

If you have questions or comments on anything relating to the book, please get in touch so we can continue the conversation. I've put several suggestions for getting in touch in the Appendix and online Resource Guide. I hope this is the start of a lively discussion. I want to hear from you—the person reading this book right now.

As with all conversations, someone has to make the first move, so let's get started.

1

Wake Up and Smell the Coffee

The sound of steaming hot water flowing through ground coffee, followed by the unmistakable aroma of Sumatra beans, tickles my brain into a foggy sense of arousal. I can taste the earthy richness inside my head, and I know it's time to start another day.

"Good morning, Margie," the soft voice of my digital assistant purrs. "This is your requested wake-up call. The time is 5:30 a.m. It's 33 degrees Fahrenheit outside right now, expected to rise to a high of 58 with partly cloudy skies. You have three appointments today and one critical task. Would you like to review them now?"

Two cups of coffee later, I'm sitting at my desk, with the day's agenda dutifully presented by my digital assistant. I find myself avoiding my noncritical task for the day—working with my new transcranial direct current stimulation (tDCS) headset, designed to transmit electrical signals to and from my brain, so that I can monitor and control my brain waves to become more productive and creative. I understand the potential benefits of this brain-machine interface (BMI), but I haven't broken this new one in yet. I put it off for now and prepare for a nice morning walk with my dogs. I remind myself that it might eventually be possible to communicate more directly with my furry loved ones if I work harder on the emerging technology waiting on my desk, but then I look into my puppy's eyes. I don't need a machine to tell me that she loves me—and is impatient to get outside.

As usual, I'm paired with my phone so I can use my speech-to-text app to outline a new online course during the walk. When I get back, I let my virtual content editor clean up my grammar and make a few suggestions to the first draft. I notice that the app has confused a couple of technical terms, so I take the time to give her feedback. Unlike a human counterpart, "she" won't make the same mistake again.

The day is also beginning for thousands of other teams of humans and machines.

Mike slips into the seat of his self-driving car and prepares for his morning commute. He knows he is supposed to pay attention to the road, but he's got an incoming text he needs to answer. Anyway, it's early and there's no one else on the road. What could possibly happen?

Ashley is fighting a cold and struggles to keep up with the timetable set for her by a computer program. She worries that her performance may be downgraded if she can't keep up.

Raul, an online news editor, plans the top stories for the day and sends the list to the "staff." An algorithm will organize the content, write the headlines, select the images, and post the stories online. He'll review them and make tweaks as needed. He sits back with a cup of coffee in his hand and looks around the newsroom. A few years ago, it would have been a noisy place, bustling with energy and crowded with reporters, news writers, graphic artists, and editors, all buzzing like bees around their computer screens with an addictive sense of urgency. Now, as he sits alone in the quiet space, there's only the gentle hum of the florescent lights and the periodic pinging sound announcing new arrivals in his inbox.

Avnish is a CFO at a Fortune 100 financial services company. While he is getting his first cup of coffee, an investment program has been selling and buying stocks and balancing the company portfolio all night, using an algorithm he helped design, even though he has no idea how it actually works. Returns are up. He dictates an update message for his boss to his personal assistant.

Mary receives a call from her doctor; the results of her mammogram, analyzed by an AI, have come back. She wonders if she can trust the results. Her doctor explains that the AI can recognize cancer much more accurately and efficiently than human analysts. He asks her if she is sitting down.

Bao is 10 years old. He's learning math at a difficulty level several years above that, however. His artificial tutor started presenting him with more challenging content after his stellar performance on several assignments and tests.

He never knows if "teacher" will be giving him a video lecture, a new game to play, or some other interesting assignment. He isn't drinking coffee, but he's so excited about school that he can't wait for another day to begin.

Alyssa is a marketing executive working on a new product launch. The new doll was designed by an AI, based on data transmitted from thousands of current dolls already in circulation. Most of the parents have no idea that the doll is capturing data about their children at play and transmitting it over the Internet.

Asha has just received a new list of candidates for the open engineering job on her team. She sighs as she goes down the list and notes that there are no women or people of color in the top 20 candidates selected by her company's résumé-screening program and wonders if she should be concerned.

Marco is a college professor considering how he will handle the results of the plagiarism alert he just received. He routinely uploads papers written by his students to be sure that their work is original. A bot searches for possible existing text that matches what the student has provided, and also identifies any passages that, based on wording and composition choices, appear to have been written by someone else. One of his best students appears to have uncharacteristically resorted to lifting large portions of her paper from other sources. The question Marco must answer is, "Why?"

Outside, on Marco's college campus, it looks like a sluggish light show. Intelligent lighting turns on and off, based on the anticipated needs of the people and applications that rely on artificial light in the early-morning hours. The system saves the college millions of dollars a year in energy bills, reduces its carbon footprint, and makes the campus safer at any time of day or night.

Minutes after lifting from the tarmac, 250 people have settled into their long flight from New York to London. The crew have activated the autopilot feature and are enjoying their first morning beverages, too.

This book is about artificial intelligence and its promise to change our lives. How many of the scenarios you've just read are examples of AI that are already in existence?

All of them.

What Is Intelligence?

You might think that the logical place to begin a discussion of artificial intelligence is with defining biological-based intelligence, particularly human intelligence, but this approach runs into problems almost immediately. Experts in psychology have yet to agree on a single definition of human intelligence (Nessier 1979). The ongoing debate includes discussions about how to measure intelligence, what behaviors demonstrate intelligence, and whether intelligence is an inherited or acquired trait.

The question of intelligence is sometimes combined or confused with the question of consciousness, particularly when combined with the concept of artificial intelligence. A full treatment of the subject could fill many books, and would venture across the fields of medicine, psychology, philosophy, ethics, and law, in addition to neuroscience and artificial intelligence. While a full discussion is well outside the scope of this book, two specific concepts are worth mentioning. They are the "hard" and "easy" problems, first identified by philosopher David Chalmers.

Chalmers correctly identified that neither consciousness nor intelligence is a single phenomenon; rather, each is a collection of behaviors. He suggested that, rather than try to understand this collection of behaviors, we begin with two questions, which he called the "hard and easy problems" (Chalmers 1995). The "easy" problem, which has proved by no means easy at all, is to explain how experience enters the brain through the senses and is coded into something that has meaning for us. The "hard" problem is understanding how to combine those sensations into a cohesive experience that is unique to each individual. If we are ever able to understand how this happens, we may be able to create a form of intelligence that demonstrates an inner life similar to our own.

As you review some of the resources provided for further reading, you may encounter these hard and easy questions. Keep in mind that, so far, science is making much more progress on the easy ones.

In his 2002 book, *Cosmos*, scientist Carl Sagan summarized the problem well. "Knowing a great deal is not the same as being smart; intelligence is not information alone but also judgment, the manner in which information is coordinated and used."

For our purposes, I like the definition put forth in the *Encyclopedia of the Human Brain*:

> "Intelligence can be defined as the ability purposively to adapt to, shape, and select real-world environments" (Sternberg and Kaufman 2002).

This definition can apply to humans as well as "intelligent machines" and gives us a place to begin talking about how the two can work together.

What Is Artificial Intelligence?

Google defines AI as "a nonhuman program or model that can solve sophisticated tasks." Notice that this definition makes no mention of mimicking human behavior or exhibiting human emotions. That's because most AI developers are not really concerned with such things. While science fiction, social media, and the popular press often focus on creating machines that relate to us in "almost human" ways, most AI professionals today are far more interested in building computerized systems that do specific, complex things. Google also leaves the definition of *sophisticated* up to us. Over time, our understanding of the tasks an AI can perform will probably evolve. It's an elegant definition and really has very little to do with human intelligence.

This definition of AI as a single-task solution is sometimes called specialized AI to distinguish it from the broader vision of general AI, or artificial general intelligence—a hypothetical, nonhuman system that is capable of performing a wide range of sophisticated tasks, from writing a symphony, to performing brain surgery, to baking a cake. General AI has yet to be achieved, and most experts believe we are very far from achieving it. It remains the stuff of dreams and nightmares, depending on your views on creating an entirely new race of sentient beings.

More recently, deep learning expert François Chollet has offered this term: cognitive automation. He explains: "Our field isn't quite 'artificial intelligence'—it's 'cognitive automation': the encoding and operationalization of human-generated abstractions, behaviors, or skills. The 'intelligence' label is a category error" (Chollet 2020).

I agree with him. Because we have failed to define human intelligence in any meaningful sense, it is pointless to try to replicate it in machines. Yet the term *AI* is unlikely to go away. So, for the time being, let's agree to use AI as a catchall term for a wide collection of use cases and programming approaches that allow us to create machine-based solutions to everyday problems. It's not very precise, but it works.

While the development of general AI remains beyond our grasp, the applications of specialized AI and cognitive automation are many, including:

- designing automobiles and airplanes to increase efficiency and reliability
- studying medical images to identify potential cancers and other illnesses
- designing new products based on the most popular features of existing ones
- matching individual cancer patients to the treatments most likely to benefit them
- analyzing large data sets to identify trends and opportunities in financial markets
- writing advertising copy and news stories
- winning sophisticated, strategy-based games against human opponents
- monitoring equipment and identifying components that are about to fail
- identifying investment opportunities based on trending patterns in global markets
- analyzing soil contents and recommending additives to increase crop yields
- finding vaccines and antidotes for new diseases
- maintaining optimal temperatures and other environmental factors for sensitive equipment
- using facial recognition to identify wanted criminals in a crowded airport
- analyzing pilot psychometrics to adjust instrument displays to account for flight fatigue.

In a field that is evolving as rapidly as AI, we can expect definitions to continue to change. Even leaders in the field struggle to define it, but, much like Supreme Court Justice Potter Stewart's explanation of obscenity, we know it when we see it. When wrapping your head around the concept, it might help to think about this explanation from business analyst David Schatsky: "AI is something machines do."

The Evolution of AI

The singularity is a term you'll find in science, science fiction, and artificial intelligence. It was coined by mathematician John von Neumann to define a theoretical moment when the artificial intelligence of computers surpasses the capacity of the human brain. The term is borrowed from physics and quantum mechanics, where the term *gravitational singularity* is used in the study of black holes. These events are all considered singular because we are unable to predict what happens next; the disruptive degree of change associated with the event is simply too great for our current body of knowledge. The term has since been appropriated by the artificial intelligence community because the creation of a machine that thinks like a human is an event that will change everything in our experience, and it is hard to imagine exactly what that new world will look like.

It is hard to say when the singularity will occur, or whether we will even recognize it when it happens. It may be that our convergence with computers will be so gradual that we will never see a sharp line, but more of a blending—like colors turning from one shade to another.

When does blue become blue-green?

When does a biological computer become a brain?

When do we stop being human and become something new?

A Brief History of AI

Humans have been using machines to augment our capabilities for a long time, so it's only natural that we've come to a point where we're looking to replicate our cognitive processes in some of those machines.

1763: Mathematician Thomas Bayes develops Bayesian inference, a decision-making technique that becomes adopted for teaching machines (and people) how to make decisions using pattern recognition and predictions based on probability.

1837: Charles Babbage invents "the analytical engine," a machine designed to perform mathematical calculations. The machine requires instructions—a program—to perform this task. His colleague Ada Lovelace writes the first program to work on his prototype. Many historians consider Babbage to be the inventor of what would later be called the computer, and Lovelace the first programmer.

1898: Inventor and electrical engineer Nikola Tesla suggests that it might be possible to build a machine that is operated through a program, using a "borrowed mind" and wireless communication.

1939: Westinghouse unveils Elektro, the first robot. This machine can deliver a recorded response to a limited number of questions, walk, smoke a cigarette, and blow up balloons. He is accompanied by his robotic dog, Sparko.

The machine is an entertaining curiosity, and not a serious attempt at artificial intelligence, but it draws attention to the potential of what would eventually become known as robotics.

1943: Warren S. McCulloch and Walter Pitts suggest that building a network of artificial neurons could create a machine that could think, using the neurons' on-or-off firing system (later binary code).

1950: With his famous opening line, "I propose the question, 'Can machines think?'" Alan Turing predicts that machines might one day mimic the cognitive functions of humans. He proposes a test to identify this phenomenon, which later becomes known as the Turing Test. While the test sidesteps the definition of intelligence altogether, Turing proposes that as long as we can be convinced that we are communicating with a person, we can consider that machine to be "intelligent."

1955: John McCarthy coins the term *artificial intelligence* at a conference convened at Dartmouth College in Hanover, New Hampshire. The conference is one of the first times that computing scholars contemplate the use of human language to program computers. By-products of this historic event include the use of neural nets to simulate human thought-processing, and the definition of *machine learning* as a "truly intelligent machine [that] will carry out activities which may best be described as self-improvement," the ability of a computer to form abstract conclusions and "orderly thinking." While the ambitious conference doesn't achieve everything it set out to do, it establishes the blueprint for progress in AI and machine learning that continue to influence the present day (McCarthy et al. 1955).

1997: IBM's "supercomputer," Deep Blue, becomes the first computer to beat a human chess champion in a match against grandmaster Garry Kasparov. Many doubt that a machine could really have performed so well and accuse IBM of cheating. The computer is "too human" to be credible.

2011: IBM Watson defeats the best human players in the popular television game show *Jeopardy!* Although a stunning achievement, the victory is nowhere near as "intelligent" as it appears. Watson is running a simple program that searches a database and provides a response faster than its human competitors. It is, however, one of the first times that a computer is able to understand and respond to human speech, paving the way for many uses of natural language processing in future applications.

2016: Russia deploys AI to successfully influence the U.S. presidential election by using bots to post comments in social media designed to mislead voters and suppress voting activity by certain types of people. This is not the first time—nor the last—that Russia and other actors have successfully influenced the outcome of an election (Kamarck 2018).

2017: DeepMind's AlphaGo caps a series of victories against humans in what is considered the most complex game in the world, Go. In a three-game match, the machine defeats world champion Ke Jie, who comments, "I thought I was very close to winning the match in the middle of the game, but that might not have been what AlphaGo was thinking" (Russell 2017).

2020: As the world scrambles to battle the devastating coronavirus pandemic, researchers around the world use machine learning to sift through mountains of research to find existing medicines that might provide an effective cure, while others put together AI programs that methodically test every chemical and compound known on Earth to see if it might be the answer. The speed, thoroughness, and efficiency of these efforts far surpass anything mere mortals could have accomplished alone. When this nightmare is finally over, many will owe their lives to an algorithm somewhere that found something that eventually led to a cure, a vaccine, or a treatment that slowed or reduced the progress of the virus.

Where Is AI in Learning and Talent Development?

The International Data Corporation (IDC) forecasts that businesses worldwide will be spending $77.6 billion on cognitive and AI systems by 2022. The highest anticipated spending is for:

- automated customer service agents
- automated threat intelligence and prevention systems
- sales process recommendations and automation of repetitive tasks
- automated preventive maintenance
- pharmaceutical research and discovery
- consumer shopping advisors and product recommendations
- digital assistants for enterprise knowledge workers
- intelligent data-processing automation.

Yet, when we look at talent development, we see that organizations are lagging behind in many respects. According to one 2020 benchmarking study, 6 percent of Fortune 500 employers include chatbots in their recruiting and onboarding experience, and 8 percent deliver recommended jobs based on candidate profiles. In a related study, 14 percent of Fortune 500 companies offer new and prospective employees semantic search capabilities (Starner 2020).

There are many notable exceptions, however, and although I cannot possibly mention them all, here are a few that come to mind.

A recent ATD conference featured a chatbot to increase participant engagement and reinforce content delivered by thought leader Bob Pike during the conference. "Bob Bot" was written by learning consultant Trish Uhl and built by AI development company Mobile Coach.

Ashok Goel, a professor at Georgia Institute of Technology, famously used an AI program to simulate a teaching assistant in 2016. "Jill Watson" supported students in the computing science master's program, answering questions about course content and clarifying assignment directions. She communicated with students through email. The original version of the program was so effective that some students nominated Jill for an award for being an outstanding TA. Today the program continues to grow, and a new, more advanced AI, Jill Social Agent, was released in 2020. Now everyone knows that Jill is an AI, and she continues to serve as an example of practical AI applied to education.

In India, educators are attempting to overcome a severe shortage of qualified teachers with innovative AI approaches. In many schools, Indian students are interacting with AI for:

- **Adaptive practice:** The algorithm selects appropriate practice activities based on individual performance to keep the student interested and challenged just enough to work hard to get to the next level without becoming discouraged.
- **Personalized content:** An AI "teacher" provides content tailored to the academic level of each student, based on previous performance data.
- **Macro diagnostics:** Algorithms predict the needs and performance of large groups of students based on historic performance data tracked during these individual engagements with AI.

I had a chance to catch up recently with Nanette Miner, author of the book *Future-Proofing Your Organization by Teaching Thinking Skills*. Her research indicates that the first skills to be replaced by AI automation will be those that are repetitive, routine, dangerous, or tedious. Replacing these jobs will free up humans to do what we do best: Create, synthesize, adapt, and envision possibilities. "This will require a major shift in the workplace as well as in education. We must encourage young minds to ask 'What if?' and 'Why not?' As adults, we must rediscover that same ability to continually learn by asking 'What if?' and 'Why not?' Stretching yourself by taking on new roles will challenge and prepare you, so that the robots can do the mundane tasks you were previously responsible for."

While I had to look far and wide for examples outside of India and China of AI in actual use in training and education today, there is much more potential than might first appear. The use cases being developed to drive performance in other industries can be easily adapted to applications for learning performance if we know where to look. And there are many voices in the talent development and education fields who speculate about a new future in which AI-enabled learning is widespread and highly effective.

Stella Collins is a learning consultant focused on the application of brain science to enhance learning and performance. We met a few years ago online and soon discovered that we're tracking many of the same trends in learning technology. I asked Stella for her thoughts about AI in our future. She replied:

> "Today, bots can share knowledge, coach you, and advise you on personalized learning choices. AI processes big data to support insights into what learning people need now and predict future requirements. In the future, AI will become more socially and emotionally intelligent, but there's a long way to go before it will replace human skills like nuance, creativity, empathy, and love. What we're more likely to do is augment our brains and bodies with AI devices, and that's not as far off as you may think."

In 2018, Ria van Dinteren, Katelijn Nijsmans, and I formed the "Brain Ladies," a global consortium of experts seeking to find new ways to deploy the converging fields of neuroscience and AI to enhance learning. In our 2018 whitepaper, *From Learning to Performance: Global Lessons From the Brain Ladies*, we point out that "advances in artificial intelligence, robotics, neuroscience, and genetics (to name a few) are transforming the way we live and learn."

There's no doubt that many of us recognize the potential of these powerful and deeply intertwined sciences and technologies, but given how many examples are already in common use in other industries, it seems as though we're falling behind. While we can't catch up overnight, we can begin by discovering how we can use AI to analyze performance data, tailor learning journeys to individual learners, and interact directly with learners in new and engaging ways.

Much as an AI can come up with a chess move or Go strategy that might never have occurred to a human, we may find that learning itself is transformed once we learn how to unleash the power of AI while we control its effects to accelerate learning and deepen retention.

Maybe we learning professionals just haven't had time to envision a world in which learning and performance are enabled by AI. Maybe we lack the funding or sponsorship to make it happen right now. Or maybe most of us are just a little afraid of it. One thing is working to our advantage in this effort. Unlike banking, marketing, financial services, customer care, agriculture, and the many other industries that are already deploying AI successfully, the learning profession is founded on many of the same principles that drive AI. That's because the science of learning and the science of building smart machines are actually part of the same multidisciplinary quest.

Did You Know That You're Already Working With AI?

The fields of artificial intelligence and talent development have been on a collision course for decades. In fact, their convergence has already occurred; it's just taking many in our profession some time to recognize this fact. From agriculture to transportation, from entertainment to medicine, from banking to social media, AI is a fundamental, disruptive technology that is changing how we humans do practically everything. And talent development is no different. From recruiting to training to compensation, AI is transforming the workplace and the role of the talent development professional. We can choose to become leaders in this transformation and prepare our organizations for the disruptions ahead, or to relegate ourselves to playing catch-up, losing ground as others take advantage of what AI has to offer to enhance learning and performance. This book, told in layman's terms and filled with practical ideas you can implement today, will help you get on the forward edge of the coming tidal wave of change.

Neuroscience and AI Are Converging

One of the most exciting developments of the last few years is the way two seemingly unrelated scientific fields, neuroscience and machine learning, have been moving toward each other. As we learn more about the brain, we're uncovering the secrets of how neurons organize themselves, communicate, recognize patterns, make decisions, form memories, and retrieve those memories. These are all functions that a self-learning AI must also perform to complete its task. The more we learn about the brain, the more insights we can apply to enhance our AI models. For example, one popular AI model is the neural network, based on the structure of the brain into layers of neurons connected in a nonlinear fashion.

In a similar way, the more sophisticated our AIs become, the greater insights we can gain about how our biological brains work. AI is being used to map the 100 billion neurons in the human brain and discover how these neurons communicate with one another.

Although *synergy* is an overused word, I can think of no better way to describe the way these two scientific fields are driving each other forward.

But we have some catching up to do first.

In Lewis Carroll's *Through the Looking-Glass*, the Red Queen tells Alice, "Now, here, you see, it takes all the running you can do, to keep in the same place. If you want to get somewhere else, you must run at least twice as fast as that!"

That's a good description of where we stand when it comes to preparing for a future that has already begun.

We must start running at least twice as fast as we can.

Chapter Summary

In this chapter we established some key terms and concepts, including:

- What is intelligence?
- What is artificial intelligence?
- Where is learning and development in the application of AI?

If you want to start exploring ways to bring the power of machine learning and artificial intelligence to your organization, try the Idea Starter in the Appendix and Resource Guide at the back of the book.

In the rest of the book, we'll look at some practical applications that are available to us today, starting with chapter 2: "Reboot Yourself With a Robot."

2

Reboot Yourself
With a Robot

When I was growing up, my favorite television program on Saturday morning was *The Jetsons*, a futuristic cartoon sitcom that promised the exciting life of tomorrow. The dad, George Jetson, is awakened every morning by an automatic process that slides him out of bed, shuffles him into the shower, and gets him ready for work while he slowly wakes up. Strangely, he still works in an office, although he commutes in a flying car and stays in touch with a videophone. Meanwhile, back at home, "Jane, his wife" is keeping the house in order (no woman's liberation was foreseen for her), with the help of a quirky AI named Rosie, who does all the housework and gets a little sassy at times. Little Jethro's best friend is Astro, an AI fashioned to look and act like a dog (except he could talk—he sounded a lot like another cartoon dog, Scooby Doo). Astro is about the only one in the family who gets any exercise, albeit he's always running in place on his little treadmill. Judy, a typical teenager, loves to shop, which oddly is done in traditional stores. Online shopping isn't dreamed of in this future. She loves to come back with arms full of packages. But the family home is equipped with an automated sidewalk, so no one has to walk very far to get anywhere. Travel to the rest of the solar system is common, the way we visit different cities today.

Two years later, a new TV program, *Lost in Space*, provided a different view of the future with B-9, a nonhumanoid robot with a passion for warning young Will Robinson of danger as the family traveled through space.

The cult sci-fi show *Doctor Who* featured many different robots, and most of them were bent on destroying the human race and taking over the Earth. But not K-9, the Doctor's robot dog. He first appeared in 1977 and made several appearances when the show returned 10 years later. K-9 was completely devoted to the Doctor, whom he called "master," finally sacrificing himself to save the Doctor and the rest of the world. As a reward, the 10th Doctor rebuilt K-9 (an advantage that robots have over us fragile humans) and left him with Sarah Jane, one of his companions, as a present. (Perhaps the most intriguing breakup gift ever.) Another robot served as the Doctor's spaceship and home. The TARDIS (time and relative dimensions in space) could fly itself, travel forward and backward in time, transform itself into any shape, and expand into an infinite number of rooms "on the inside." The TARDIS also developed deep romantic feelings for the Doctor and was jealous of his human companions.

Fast-forward to 2001, when *Star Trek: Enterprise* introduced us to Lieutenant Commander Data, a super-intelligent AI who is a member of the crew in 2151. Data also had an evil twin, Lore, who learned his evil ways by studying humans. Data had to save the humans many times and was sometimes a bit smug and condescending about his superior talents. But deep down, he desperately wanted to be more human, trying to fall in love, tell jokes, and feel empathy for others. Some would say he is the most authentically human member of the crew.

In 2016, HBO launched the series *Westworld,* based on the film by the same name. In this dystopian future, a high-tech amusement park is populated by robotic "hosts" who are programmed to satisfy the deepest fantasies of their human "guests." When some of the robots begin to develop consciousness, all hell breaks loose.

In pre-COVID 2020, I was driving back home from a real-life meeting in downtown Phoenix when I was suddenly surrounded by a small fleet of all-white economy cars. My first impression was that they were rentals, being returned from somewhere. But the cars were somehow "behaving" differently. Their movements weren't erratic or dangerous, but I noticed a precision in their movements as a group, as though they were performing a water ballet on the highway at precisely 55 miles an hour. It became clear that they were trying to get me out of the center of their little dance, so I obliged by slowing down. As the last car sped past me, I noticed the bumper sticker on the back. I had been surrounded by a test fleet of self-driving cars. Humans were on board, of course, as a fail-safe, but the movements I witnessed were the result of driving algorithms meant to promote public safety.

We're still waiting for our flying cars, but we have videophones and portable computers in the palms of our hands. There are also robots among us, even if we don't know it.

Are You a Robot or a Bot?

You'll often find the terms *robot*, *bot*, and *AI* used interchangeably, even in this book. While it is often overlooked in the popular press, there actually is a difference. I like the definition provided by CodeBots.com (Tansey 2017): "Our definition of robots and bots is that they are both programmable machines that can automatically execute actions. There are those with bodies (robots) and those that are simply programs (bots)."

For the purposes of this book, it often doesn't matter if the programmable machine has a body or not. My focus is on what these machines can do to enhance learning and performance. Thus, I tend to use *bot*, but will occasionally use *robot*, if that term makes more sense in context.

Will You Be Replaced by a Robot?

Will you be replaced by a robot? I'd like to assure you that the answer is "no," but the truthful answer is "maybe." Oxford economist Carl Benedikt Frey predicts that 47 percent of jobs could be replaced by automation in the near future (Frey and Osborne 2013). There is even a companion website to Frey's paper that lets you submit your job to see if the paper makes any prediction about your chances of being replaced by a robot. However, based on trends from the past few years, it's far more likely that you will soon have robot employees and colleagues who expand and transform your work life, rather than replacing you altogether. This is because the state of AI, even at its most advanced, still needs human direction to be most effective. And that's good news for us "biological machines" (LTEN 2019).

For example, in the healthcare industry, some providers are testing robots that can conduct a conversation with elderly or other at-risk patients, to remind them to take their medication, offer to check their blood pressure, recommend exercise and diet tips, and other basic services. Other applications have proven that AIs can identify cancer by reviewing a patient's scan faster and more accurately than a trained human. This application frees the humans for more nuanced analysis that can't be resolved by a machine.

What would you like to do faster or more accurately, or get out of doing at all? Think about all the things you do in your job and make a list of tasks that are repetitive, routine, or require minimal creativity to accomplish. To give you some ideas, here's my list:

- reading and responding to most emails (not yours, of course!)
- managing my calendar
- proofreading content
- searching for information
- managing my to-do list
- preparing and sending invoices
- following up on past-due payments (again, not yours, of course!)
- keeping track of business and personal financial records
- updating my website and posting on social media.

Depending on your role, your list may be different, but I'm willing to bet that you can identify at least a few tasks that could be—and perhaps should be—done by someone else. But in today's world there is really no "someone else" for most of us. Many L&D professionals are sole contributors in their organization. If they manage a team, those people have their own work to do. Productivity experts are fond of telling us to delegate whenever possible, but for most of us, this simply isn't an option. When we look around us, there is no one to delegate the work to.

What if you could outsource some of those lower-value tasks? What would that look like for you?

Learning technology expert JD Dillon suggests several applications for AI-enabled talent development, including a few opportunities for automation that might surprise you. I've expanded on his list and added a few of my own (Dillon 2020).

Hire an Assistant

You may not be able to hire your own personal assistant, but you can "hire" a digital personal assistant right now. Your new co-worker will probably require some training, but with some effort and patience, you'll soon be delegating more simple tasks to your assistant, such as relying on it to tell you what deliverables are due today and set your schedule. Apple users have learned to rely on Siri for everything from reading their email, to taking dictation, to even making dinner reservations. The simple voice-activated interface makes it easy to communicate with virtual assistants and can help you free up some time for more complex tasks—plus keep you from forgetting your mother-in-law's birthday. (If you "hire" an Alexa for this purpose, she'll also be more than happy to shop for you and order Mom the perfect gift on Amazon. She'll even have it shipped and gift-wrapped, with a lovely card enclosed.) Additional tasks your administrative assistant can do for you today include:

- Draft meeting agendas based on content in an email.
- Proofread your emails and documents.
- Schedule meetings across multiple calendars and send invitations at times when all parties are available.
- Summarize and read the news to you.
- Read your email to you and take dictation to respond.
- Remind you of important tasks and deadlines.
- Tell you what movies are appearing at a theater near you and buy tickets.
- Track your exercise and sleep patterns and recommend healthier habits.
- Tell you a joke, play your favorite music, or sing you a song to brighten your day.
- Greet you with a cheery "Good morning" at the start of every day and turn on the coffee machine.

Sound too good to be true? There are certainly some challenges to working with a digital assistant, so be prepared for the unexpected. I have a friend who is still trying to get Siri to distinguish between his brother and his brother-in-law, both named Bob. If he doesn't carefully phrase his commands, he ends up "Siri dialing" the wrong person. My editor has a Google smart speaker. One day, she was watching a YouTube video of Patrick Mahomes showing off his high-tech "smart home." When the quarterback said "Hey, Google," my editor's machine responded.

Like any new "employee," your assistant will need to be trained if you want to enjoy a productive relationship with it.

If you haven't experimented with a digital assistant, this could be an excellent way to dip your toe into the AI experience that many of your learners already enjoy. If you own a smartphone for personal or professional use, you already hold one of these digital assistants in your hand, even if you've never asked it to do anything. I encourage you to experiment with ways to become more productive and efficient in your daily routine.

Once you start using your digital assistant, it's not much of a leap to imagine practice applications that will support learning and performance support. One of my clients uses the proprietary software on their employees' company phones to provide just-in-time answers to questions on procedures, company policy, technical processes, and more. It's like having a coach standing right by you while you do your job. It can reduce errors, reduce downtime, and improve productivity.

Most of your learners likely already have smartphones and other devices that can access a digital assistant. Whether this is a company-provided phone or you work in a BYOD (bring your own device) environment, you may be able to use these digital assistant programs to deliver short, in-the-moment learning activities such as:

- reminders for class schedules and due dates for prework, homework, or assessments
- review questions to reinforce content from training
- access to job aids and other performance support documents on the job
- fun facts or tips to keep things interesting.

Sound like something you'd like to try? Selecting the right digital assistant for you is beyond the scope of this book. (Besides, the details would probably change by our date of publication.) Your choice for your digital assistant will probably depend on which platform is most available and comfortable for you. Here's a list of some popular options.

Platform	Assistant
Apple	Siri
Android	Google Now
Microsoft	Cortana
Facebook Messenger	Facebook M
Amazon Echo	Alexa

Hire a Junior Writer

You may think that only a human can write compelling, accurate content for training, but robot writers have been employed by news outlets and online marketing companies for years. In fact, there's a good chance that you've read news stories written without any human intervention and you didn't even know it. Here are a few of the major outlets that regularly use AI programs to produce at least some of their content: *Forbes,* the *Washington Post,* the *Los Angeles Times,* and the Associated Press. It's not as simple as just writing a program and unleashing it to produce tomorrow's headlines, however. "The work of journalism is creative, it's about curiosity, it's about storytelling, it's about digging and holding governments accountable, it's critical thinking, it's judgment—and that is where we want our journalists spending their energy," said Lisa Gibbs, the director of news partnerships for the AP (Martin 2019). In most cases, AI can be used in a more supportive role, like a junior reporter who is learning the ropes from a more experienced news writer. Journalists can be freed from the necessary but sometimes time-consuming tasks of gathering and interpreting data, identifying trends, validating sources, and locating contact information for subject matter experts (SMEs). As Gibbs says, the use of AI frees human journalists to do what they do best, by letting AI do what it does best. The two skill sets, at least today, are quite different.

What would it be like to have an AI write your learning content? Setting these concerns aside for a moment, let's think of all the content your organization puts out on a daily basis. The Internet is growing by a staggering amount every day, and your company intranet is just a smaller example of the same phenomenon. A content development bot could help you by:

- delivering a daily report on key organizational metrics so you can monitor trends and make recommendations to stakeholders
- identifying top performers and strugglers on the job, so you can deliver a learning solution that keeps top performers from getting bored and helps low performers improve their skills in real time
- creating a first-pass storyboard based on SME-provided content so you can get some initial responses before you invest too much time perfecting a design that must be approved by others
- drafting one-page product guides from larger documents like manuals and whitepapers
- populating presentation slides from a script, news article, or blog post for your review
- inserting or recommending images for a presentation based on keywords in the content
- using a template to design a webpage or convert classroom content into self-paced e-learning
- identifying broken links and page issues on your intranet and e-learning pages, attempting to fix them, and letting you know which ones need your personal attention

- automatically updating learning content for routine items, such as product changes, that can be identified by constantly monitoring all corporate communication
- running reports on learner activity, satisfaction, performance, and other key performance indicators and producing attractive dashboards or spreadsheets to present the data to your stakeholders.

Translate Your Training Almost Instantly

If you're working in a global organization, or your learners come to you speaking and reading a variety of different languages, chances are you're already outsourcing translation services to make your content more relevant and accessible to your learning audience. In today's global and digital workplace, where learners can be based anywhere, the written and spoken language of training and education has grown increasingly complex. Training content may be created by human content developers on one side of the globe and consumed by learners all over the world. Online schools and universities face the same challenge—how to efficiently and effectively translate content without changing its meaning. This means that the translation program must not only perform a literal translation from the words of one language to another; it must be able to recognize and adjust for cultural differences, local references, idiom, and slang, which can change the way a learner interprets what they read or hear.

As anyone who has watched a foreign film with captions will attest, translating from one language to another is not a simple word-for-word replacement. While babies learn their native language with relative ease, today's AI is still challenged by nuances that come easily to the human brain. For example, an AI might not be able to parse the difference between *read* (present tense) and *read* (past tense) and many other meanings that are dependent on context.

The challenge for determining how well AI is doing with human language is that the humans are serving as the judges—and we keep changing the rules. In his book, *The Measure of All Minds: Evaluating Natural and Artificial Intelligence* (2017), Dr. José Hernández-Orallo writes, "AI measurement suffers from a moving-target phenomenon." In other words, as soon as AI gets good at doing something, we humans raise the bar and no longer find the previous level of achievement interesting. Thus, it never seems to get quite good enough, because we humans know that the effort was generated by a machine. Hernández-Orallo proposes that a better means of measurement might be to flip the equation: to measure the performance of an AI by the effort required by the human to detect it. Using this yardstick, one only has to play around with Google Translate to see two different answers to the same question. Although AI has come a long way in the ability to translate human speech or text, it still has a long way to go.

One of the most interesting developments to me is that most AIs seem to do better learning on their own; the less we tell them in advance, the better and faster they seem to learn. In this respect, the two neural networks (human versus machine) are quite similar. Learning through free-flowing experience is often more effective and creates a deeper and broader "understanding" than teaching through lecture or hard-programming.

If you are using a translation service today that is powered by human translators, chances are they are leveraging artificial intelligence for more basic applications, with a human reviewer who can add the nuance and correct anything that doesn't quite hit the right note for a human audience. Each time the human reviewer enters a correction, the program learns from this experience, so these targeted applications can only get better.

As long as you get a quality result, to me there is really no reason to debate whether the result is produced completely by the algorithm, or whether it represents a collaboration between human and machine.

Translation is a perfect example of how targeted AIs have already entered the workforce as virtual colleagues and assistants, rather than competitors for our jobs. Just as a different generation had to learn how to use computers and the Internet to do their work in new ways, today's learning managers need to plan for how they can incorporate a new array of helpers to make life easier and drive performance—for their learners and for themselves.

Curate Your Content

Curation has become a popular topic in learning and development circles. It's a term borrowed from the art world, where the role of a curator is to collect works that support a gallery's theme or mission and then present these works in meaningful ways to the public. The role of the curator in L&D is similar. We package content from a wide variety of sources and organize it in a way that makes it more accessible to the learner. By employing artificial intelligence, you can create an interface that tailors the recommendation to each learner, based on individual needs, requirements, and interests. The sources for this information may include a learning management system (LMS), YouTube, Vimeo, online third-party courses from providers like Coursera or LinkedIn Learning, books, magazines, blogs, and other sources. Many companies are looking at curation as a powerful way to leverage existing content in engaging new ways. With an intelligent curation engine, you can delegate the difficult and sometimes tedious work of going through thousands of digital artifacts to find the content that will be most valuable to your learning audience. It would take an army of humans to do this, and it likely wouldn't be as fast or as thorough as a well-designed AI. We'll talk more about curation solutions in chapter 4.

Manage Course Registration and Payment

If you provide courses to a large number of people, the registration process could quickly become a nightmare. And if you charge for those courses, you have to factor in the complexity of conducting e-commerce securely. Course registration, payment collection, fulfillment, and reporting can all be handled by a number of programs that are available today. You may also find that e-commerce is an option that is available on your LMS. Even if you never intend to charge for your courses, registration and delivery can be a logistical challenge. This might be a perfect opportunity to implement some simple and targeted intelligence to do the work for you.

Get Ready for the Digital Employee

These examples of targeted AI demonstrate that smart machines are already entering the workforce as virtual colleagues and assistants, rather than competitors for our jobs. As a talent development professional, you have the opportunity to make yourself more productive and efficient by using a variety of these bots, and you can put yourself in a position to lead the way in the implementation and development of these tools in the workplace.

For many professions, artificial intelligence will introduce much-needed help in the form of smart robots and programs that support or augment the human side of work. For example, IT professionals who augment their surveillance with AI can gain 20 times more effective attack-surveillance coverage than traditional methods, allowing them to find and remedy critical security vulnerabilities 40 percent faster (Ciccarelli 2020).

In many countries, including the U.S., 2020 began with a serious labor shortage. Employers struggled to fill jobs due to low single-digit unemployment and other factors (Lowrey 2018). However, in response to the COVID-19 pandemic and the resulting downturn in the global economy, many companies were suddenly unable to maintain their operating expenses, laying off large portions of their workforce or cutting hours and wages. Consulting powerhouse

McKinsey & Company warns about the post-pandemic "next normal," a period during which nearly every business will be disrupted by the necessity of responding to and recovering from COVID-19, resulting in a major shift in how we conduct business at all levels. As learning professionals, we must arm ourselves with the agility and business acumen to be ready to support a number of possible "nexts," including:

- An increased focus on delivering education via distance learning
- An increased reliance on automation in the form of drones and robots to deliver basic goods and services
- A new way to provide healthcare, which may include automated solutions, such as tracking apps, chatbots, and virtual doctor appointments

In March 2020, McKinsey analysts Kevin Sneader and Shubham Singhal wrote:

It is increasingly clear our era will be defined by a fundamental schism: the period before COVID-19 and the new normal that will emerge in the post-viral era: the "next normal." In this unprecedented new reality, we will witness a dramatic restructuring of the economic and social order in which business and society have traditionally operated. . . . More simply put, it's our turn to answer a question that many of us once asked of our grandparents: What did you do during the war?

The good news for us humans is that we're supremely prepared for this challenge through thousands of years of evolution.

André Vermeulen is one of the pioneers in the application of brain science to enhance learning and development. His company, Neuro-Link, is a boutique consultancy specializing in the neuroscience of performance optimization and neuro-agility. Vermeulen recently reminded me that learning is "the DNA of the mind. It is the key to not only mankind's survival, but also to our competitiveness, employability, prosperity, and success. It is therefore essential to optimize all the brain-based elements that will influence the ease, speed, and flexibility with which we learn, think, and process information." You can learn more about his ideas on his website, provided in the references.

Our brain is the most complex single object known to humankind and it is constantly rewiring itself in response to new information. We are constantly learning; we simply can't help ourselves. Learning is our superpower. By teaching learners how to fine-tune their learning skills, we can help them keep up with the accelerating pace of change, integrate new concepts and processes into their daily routines, and develop new skills to help them continue to advance in their careers. Those same skills will enable all of us, as learning professionals, to succeed and thrive as well.

Throughout history, the development of new technologies has turned complex trades into routine tasks. When the automobile was first introduced, most people believed that you needed a skilled driver to operate and maintain it. Now we consider that process so routine that learning to drive is a standard rite of passage for most teenagers today, and we're already outsourcing the task to digital employees in the form of "self-driving cars." According to a recent study by LinkedIn Learning, the introduction of AI into the workplace will require almost everyone to acquire new skills. What we once called "soft skills" or "people skills" make the top of the list, only now these skills will include ways to collaborate with machines (Berger 2019).

Beware the Uncanny Valley

You may have noticed that I sometimes refer to artificial intelligence applications with the personal pronouns *he* and *she*. That's because it's natural for us to assign human characteristics to the apparent "behavior" of animals and machines. Our brains are prewired for social interaction. It's an evolutionary response to our earlier environments, which were so dangerous that banding together was the only way for the species to survive. This urge is so compelling that we look for social connections where they may not really exist. Having close relationships with our pets is not such a stretch, especially in light of increasing evidence that their brains are structured much like ours and that they have an inner life that has many cognitive and emotional correlates to our own.

What may be more surprising to you is that we can also form deep and complex attachments with machines. In fact, we've been doing it for centuries. Have you ever given your car a name? Or told a friend that your P.C., phone, golf club, or other inanimate object doesn't "like" you today? It could be just a colorful way of expressing yourself, but it is often something more. Our machines are psychological and physical extensions of ourselves. They take us places we couldn't go on our own, make us safer and more dangerous, and give us new ways to engage with the world and ourselves. In the movie *Castaway,* Tom Hanks befriends a soccer ball that has washed up on the beach along with the rest of the debris from his wrecked plane. The longer he stays alone on the island, the more he depends on his friendship with "Wilson" to keep him sane, or at least get him through another lonely day.

Humans have been falling in love with technology since the first time someone picked up a rock and reimagined it as a tool. That person soon discovered that a rock can be a lifesaving device to build a home or prepare food, or a weapon to harm another being. That dichotomy has been the story of our conflicted relationship with our machines ever since.

While investing our machines with personality might be fun, it has a darker side. We can sometimes become overly dependent on them, replacing genuine social contact with the appearance of a social world on our devices. As natural language processing continues to improve, our AIs will only become more and more like people, making it easier to interact with their powerful capabilities and creating more potential for confusing our all-too-human brains.

An interesting phenomenon we'll likely encounter is called the uncanny valley. AI pioneer Masahiro Mori demonstrated that as robots (AIs in physical form) become more and more human in appearance, we are at first engaged, even charmed. But this pleasant reaction continues only as long as we are able to differentiate the experience from a human-to-human interaction. At some point, the appearance, voice, and behavior can cross a line, appearing almost too human. As *IEEE Spectrum* author Rina Diane Caballar (2019) puts it, "There's something about it being almost human but not quite that can make people uneasy." Mashiro's theory further posits that at some point the robot may become so humanlike that our revulsion evaporates and we begin to enjoy the interaction again, forgetting that our companion is, in fact, artificial.

Think about how you would react if your cat or dog suddenly started talking to you in perfect sentences. It might sound pretty cool, but it would probably be truly frightening if it happened tomorrow.

Experiencing the Uncanny Valley

Trish O'Connor, the owner of Epiclesis Consulting and its new publishing arm, Epiclesis Press (www.EpiclesisPress.com), is developing a new interactive journaling aid that brings together her computer programming skills, spirituality, and principles from the art of magic in what she calls "cyberillusionism." Intended as a tool for spiritual reflection such as dream analysis, her algorithms create the eerie illusion of a conversation with a spiritual director named "Chris."

I wanted to try it out, so here is an excerpt from my own conversation with her "beta" version of the bot (Figure 2-1).

Figure 2-1. Example Bot Script

Chris	Me
Hello, I'm Chris. So you want to talk about a dream?	Yes
Why do you suppose this dream is so important to you?	Because I was suddenly very panicky. In a flash I realized I hadn't attended class all term and the final was today.
What happened?	I thought I knew a shortcut through the woods, so I headed back to class. Inside my head, I was calculating the time. "Forty minutes to make it," that sort of thing.
I find the timing interesting, but you tell me …	Well, I've been working hard to finish my book for ATD. There's a lot of moving parts.
That sounds like a piece of the puzzle.	I don't see how.
I think you know better than that.	Well, after that dream, I blocked off time on my calendar to finish my book.
Let's go back to the dream.	I was carrying a book. I was clutching it tightly. At the time, I thought it was a textbook, but now I think it might have been the book I'm writing for ATD.
So what might that symbolize?	The dream is about my work, my reputation.

For me, this experience felt very strange, yet quite comfortable at the same time. I also felt that I gained real insight into my dream and the state of my mind from the exercise. If you want to have your own uncanny valley experience, visit the Resource Site.

Prepare to Be "Creeped Out" a Bit

Our applications of AI become will more sophisticated and more general in nature. We will need to consider how to help users adapt to the potential creepiness of the interaction, so that they can get through the uncanny valley and enjoy the benefits the application is designed to provide.

As we prepare to bring AI into daily life, the temptation to imbue these learning machines and systems with imagined personalities and intents will be powerful, perhaps irresistible. As a talent development professional, you will not be entirely immune to this human trait, but you can be aware of it and prepare to resist it in yourself while you help others maintain a boundary between the AI that helps them do their jobs and the human beings in their lives. But maybe that's OK, and we will interact better with machines that feel like colleagues.

Has COVID-19 Accelerated Investments in AI?

In 2020, it is impossible to discuss the future without considering the impact of the COVID-19 pandemic. While the final chapter in the story of the human race and its battle with this deadly disease has yet to be written, the opening paragraphs suggest a time of increased awareness of and investment in artificial intelligence, if only because it is being used so freely in the rush to find a cure or vaccine. The work being done around the world to track the spread of the disease and test potential treatments or vaccines has been driven by machine learning, and is showing the world the enormous potential for AI to recognize patterns and solve problems faster than humans could ever achieve.

While this massive effort is under way, AI itself is evolving. By its very nature, an AI gets better with use. The data scientists, programmers, and cognitive scientists engaged in pointing the power of AI toward a virus are learning new techniques every day. These techniques will translate into advancements in medicine, technology, computer science, pharmaceuticals, and other industries. But more importantly, the work being done by the AI community to fight COVID-19 today is making us all a whole lot smarter. And we'll be able to apply those solutions to new problems as soon as we're able to change our focus. At the same time, decision makers who aren't very educated about AI today will be much more familiar with how it works, its limitations, and its potential. From where I sit, it seems likely that the post-pandemic world is a world driven by AI—perhaps even sooner than predicted before a global crisis forced us to seize the most powerful tool we have to fight our most dangerous foe.

Summary: Get Ready to Change

In this opening chapter, we introduced additional key terms, including:

- machine learning
- the singularity
- general intelligence.

We also talked about some simple, practical ways that you can begin engaging with AI today, by using technology readily available to you as a consumer with a smartphone. We explored a few use cases for AI in the workplace, specifically related to our field of talent development. And we peeked a bit into the near future, as we begin to move from hypothetical use cases to living examples of these use cases in practice. Along the way, it was impossible to discuss our present or our future without touching on the impact of COVID-19. The full details of that event in our history have not been written, but it is safe to say that we have been changed by our shared ordeal.

We addressed a question that many of us ask when we think about AI and automation: "Will I be replaced by a robot?" If your livelihood depends on performing manual, repetitive tasks, the answer to that question is "probably." But since you're reading this book, I can make some assumptions about the work you are doing today and can give you a different answer. It is much more likely that your work will be transformed by an army of smart machines. You will likely find yourself collaborating with machines, if you aren't already. Nearly every job has some tasks that are routine and require minimal cognitive effort to accomplish. Intelligent machines can take over these tasks, so that we can focus on those tasks that require human involvement—creativity, judgment, compassion. Parkinson's Law says that the amount of work in an organization expands to fill the available time. So even if you succeed in delegating all your current duties to a new team of digital employees, you'll still find plenty of work to do— it will just be *different* work.

Working with these smart machines can do more than solve scientific puzzles like COVID-19. It can move the organization—and the people within it—into new levels of insight and performance.

If you're interested in engaging some of the simple programs mentioned here to streamline your work, you'll find updated information, tips, and training on the Resource Site.

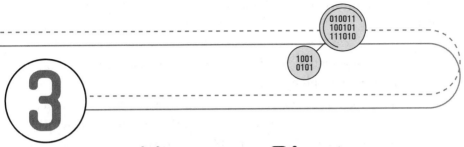

Have a Chat
With a Machine

A few years ago, I was curious about something new I was seeing as a consumer. My bank, Amazon, and many other e-commerce sites were moving to automated "virtual assistants," rather than using live operators, to answer routine questions. My bank had sent me a letter, announcing what a great new thing this would be, because I could get answers to my questions on demand, without waiting for the next available agent. So, I got online and tried it out. The first few questions went well. I played nice with "Alice," asking her questions that I knew she could answer. Her response was nearly immediate, every time. Finally, I decided to test the bot with a question that wasn't in the script. "Are you real?" I asked her. "Certainly. I'm helping you, aren't I?" She was quite right. So I tried to trip her up again. "Are you a human being?" I knew that she was not. She replied with a question, "Does it matter?"

I started implementing chatbots into my learning solutions for my clients in 2016 and made several joint presentations at ATD TechKnowledge and other venues with my friend "eLearning Joe" Ganci around the same time. Neuroscience tells us that as long as the responses are sufficiently authentic, it *doesn't matter* to your brain. Chatbots are no longer a novelty. They are so common in our daily lives that we usually pay them no attention at all. Let's look at one man's typical day.

Mike is an accountant at a Fortune 500 company. Before work begins, he checks his retirement fund. The virtual assistant helps him review his balance and play some "what if" scenarios with his investment options and retirement timeline. Next, he logs on to his employer's virtual private network (VPN) to start his work-from-home day. When he logs in, he lands on the intranet homepage, where a cheery bot welcomes him by name and asks, "How can I help you?" He types in "vacation days" and the bot responds with a link that provides general information about how the company allocates time off. That isn't what he wanted, so he types a new question. "How many vacation days do I have left?" The bot answers, "You have 10 days left in this calendar year. Would you like to schedule them now?" "No thanks," he replies, unaware of the needless effort to be polite to a machine. "Is there anything else I can help you with?" "Not now," he replies and logs in to his inbox.

His company uses Google for their email and documents, and they have set up a Google Hangouts bot. "What's my schedule today?" Mike asks. The bot presents his calendar in visible form, highlighting a few places where two calls overlap. "Cancel webinar," he says. "Which one?" Google replies. "Financial services best practices at 10 a.m." "Cancel financial services best practices at 10, right?" "Yes." "Canceled. Is there anything else?" "Not right now. Thanks." (Mike was raised to be polite to everyone.)

After lunch, Mike notices that the network has slowed to a crawl. He accesses the Help Desk page on the intranet and is greeted by another bot. "How can I help you?" it begins. Mike describes the issue. "I need to connect you to a live agent for assistance. May I schedule a callback for you?" "Yes." The bot presents several available slots and Mike picks one that works for his schedule. An hour later, he receives a call as scheduled and the issue is resolved with the help of a human agent.

After a long day, Mike takes a course online. He's working toward an MBA, with financial assistance from his company. The school offers a "Student Assistant" bot that performs many of the services that once were provided by human academic advisors. While he's waiting for tonight's lecture to begin, Mike explores some options for his next course with the bot and schedules his next class.

After class, it's finally time for Mike to relax. He's planning a skiing trip soon, so he checks his favorite weather bot to learn where conditions will be best next week. He opens a music app on his phone and asks the bot to find that new song he heard yesterday, so he can add it to a playlist. Mike doesn't know the title or artist, but he hums a few notes and the bot finds it.

Mike never once told himself that the bots he engaged weren't "real"; he only needed to be connected to a human assistant once. The era of chatbots is here. Talent development just hasn't caught up yet.

As we've seen, specialized AI succeeds in performing a single sophisticated or complex task or related set of tasks. So far, this is the only type of AI that has been built. You don't have to wait for the far-off day when general AI is available to start using AI to enhance learning. You can begin today with a much narrower focus and still achieve powerful results. One place to get started is the chatbot.

You may have interacted with a chatbot behaving like a customer service agent, for example, or used Google's "smart reply" to handle email more efficiently. Microsoft displays gentle contextual reminders on how to best use its Office software using AI. Many other applications work beneath the surface of our digital lives; some collect data to help auto manufacturers decide what features will be most popular on next year's models, or tell Amazon what products we might want to buy based on our browsing history. All these examples not only make life easier for the user—they change behavior. And behavior change means that learning is taking place.

Natural Language Processing and the Illusion of Conversation

A key component of the AI experience is natural language processing (NLP). NLP allows us to interact with a computer, system, or program through speech or ordinary text, without the need to translate our instructions, requests, or input into programming languages or code.

The Trouble With Acronyms—NLP vs. NLP

The trouble with using acronyms as stand-ins for technical terms is that sometimes we create confusion rather than clarity. A case in point is the confusion I sometimes see around natural language processing (NLP) vs. neurolinguistic programming (also NLP). Natural language processing is an important feature of some artificial intelligence programs, as I've just described. Neurolinguistic programming is a collection of quackery and pseudoscience that purports to give you influence over the behavior of others and yourself by choosing certain words that somehow create behavioral programs in the brain. Although widely debunked in peer-reviewed journals, the practice continues to have fervent followers and occasionally trips up even the best-educated learning professional.

In this book, anytime I am talking about NLP, I am always referring to natural language processing.

This single advance in computer programming is responsible for creating much of our digital experience. Without NLP, you couldn't ask your digital assistant to make dinner reservations, program your phone to wake you up in the morning, or conduct a search online without knowing computer code. NLP puts the power of computing into the hands of the general user, allowing us to use computers so seamlessly today that we scarcely think about the ease with which we are "communicating" with a machine.

What Is a Chatbot?

A chatbot is not a website, a learning management system, a performance support system, e-learning, or an app, but it can enhance the user experience when paired with each of these more familiar learning technologies.

I define a chatbot as a customized user interface (UI) designed to deliver content and collect information through a direct, two-way conversation with the user. The two sides of the "conversation" can be delivered audibly, via human or simulated speech, or via keyboarded text.

You've probably used a chatbot and not even thought much about it. Online shopping sites, financial service companies, and software help desks all employ chatbots to provide basic customer services. The fields of education and corporate training have been slower to adopt the technology, but that is starting to change. For example, the online course provider Udacity is using NLP to make personalized recommendations to learners, while some online colleges are using it to take the place of a teaching assistant.

It is important to note that chatbots are not necessarily examples of AI. Simple chatbots with limited programming do not have to be particularly intelligent to be effective. While a "smart" bot can interpret the meaning and context of a request from a wide variety of human words and styles of expression, a "dumb" bot will be limited to the responses provided in its programming. Still, a dumb bot can serve many useful purposes, but sooner or later users will arrive at the point where they get a default response like, "I'm sorry, I don't know. Let me refer you to someone who can help."

While even the simplest bot can be very effective in handling routine requests quickly and just-in-time, the true power of a chatbot lies in the bot's ability to analyze the learner's own language and respond in kind. The result is an experience that feels like a conversation because, well, *it is*.

Shannon Tipton and "Conversational Learning"

Shannon Tipton is the "Chief Learning Rebel" and founder of Learning Rebels. I had been following her blog for years when I finally had the chance to meet her face-to-face at a conference in Berlin where I spoke about how to embrace disruptive technologies. Shannon has coined the term *conversational learning*, updating the Socratic method for today's digital learning experience. I interviewed her about conversational learning and how it relates to the use of chatbots. "These days," she said, "the modern workforce expects to be able to get the training they need, when they need it. In an age when most people have their phones at their fingertips, a well-designed chatbot provides access to a toolbox of resources and solutions are only a text message away. This is what conversational learning is all about, allowing the people in your business to receive help when the person needs it and when the business needs them to have it all at their fingertips."

For the purposes of this book, any reference to "chatbot" is to an intelligent, AI-powered program using conversational input and output.

When you are "speaking" with something, your brain is hardwired to conclude that you are speaking with an equal—a being capable of responding back with its own independent thoughts. The fact that we know that general AI isn't possible doesn't prevent us from feeling that we are having a "real" conversation. Like any other illusion, we can't help seeing it, even when we know it isn't true.

Although this phenomenon has serious ethical considerations for the implementation of AI in our lives, it also presents some exciting opportunities, particularly as we look for ways to use AI to enhance learning and performance, including:

- interactive coaching programs that respond to learner questions
- more realistic branching scenarios for blended and e-learning programs
- learning management systems (LMSs) that make personalized recommendations for each learner
- data analysis to identify learner reaction, achievement, and preferences in near real time
- contextual performance and process suggestions based on actions the user is taking at the moment.

Figure 3-1 depicts a real-life example of a chatbot, described in the following sidebar.

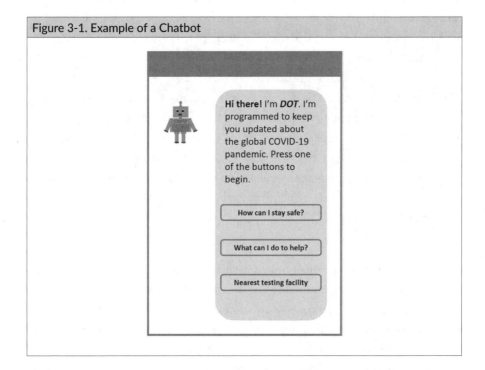

Figure 3-1. Example of a Chatbot

A Trusted Friend in a Time of Crisis

While I was writing this book, the coronavirus took hold of the world, spreading illness, death, and panic to almost every corner of the globe. Health workers and first responders struggled to care for the increasing number of victims. News outlets struggled to provide current, reliable information on the spread of the virus and how to stay safe. And every one of us struggled with sorting through the mountain of data coming at us from all sides and determining what we could believe. Much of the information online was confusing, or even plain false.

Many organizations and individuals jumped in to try to offer advice, free services, and guidelines for staying safe during this frightening time. From tips for putting training and school courses online to ideas for having fun at home, everyone seemed to have an opinion. Like many of you, I was deeply engaged with "virtualizing" training that had been conducted face-to-face prior to the pandemic, responding to the urgent needs of schools, universities, and corporate training departments. In the course of that struggle, I was looking for a way to add value. I didn't want to be just another voice with practical suggestions about what you could or should do to keep your business running. I felt that there were plenty of voices delivering that information in highly credible ways.

However, I saw a gap in delivering up-to-date information about personal safety, the stuff that would keep our loved ones healthy and alive through the pandemic. I was already working with Mobile Coach to develop a series of low-price "semi-custom" chatbots to support a series of training needs, such as onboarding, new manager training, and sales enablement. We realized that one of the most valuable things we could offer is a way for people to ask a trusted advisor about the crisis and know that they are receiving the best answers available at the time.

The result was a chatbot that pulled data from live feeds from the Centers for Disease Control and Prevention (CDC) and the World Health Organization (WHO). By tracking the most common answers and linking to the most up-to-date information from two reliable sources, we made our little contribution to the world in a time of crisis. Engaging a chatbot feels like a conversation because it is; I like to think that we gave the thousands of users who found our little bot some valuable information and a bit of comfort in a time of terror.

A Brief History of Chatbots

While they have gained a great deal of traction lately, chatbots have been around since the early days of the computer, when theorists like Alan Turing suggested that humans would eventually succeed in building a computer that was indistinguishable from a human being.

By the 1970s, a nonintelligent version of a chatbot answered almost every customer service number, screening the call through a series of menu options designed to direct the call to the most efficient resource.

As computing power and programming techniques advanced, it became possible to build computer programs that began to approximate human conversation within narrow constraints, such as the IBM AI that defeated human competitors in the popular TV game *Jeopardy!* Today we're accustomed to talking to our phones and other devices using virtual assistant software. These interactions have become so seamless that many users refer to Siri, Alexa, or Cortana as "she," and ascribe personality traits to the program.

Why Are Chatbots So Popular?

As a result of evolution, humans are predisposed to interact with one another. Social connection triggers the reward circuit in the brain, making us seek out engagement and connection with other humans. Done well, the chatbot brings increased learner engagement to an automated learning experience, creating the same response in the brain that is triggered through social interaction with other people.

Anthropomorphism is the human tendency to ascribe human behaviors and emotions to nonhuman creatures and inanimate objects. This tendency has been studied extensively, particularly in virtual environments. The more "human" we perceive the entity on the other side of the conversation to be, the more engaging, interesting, and trustworthy we perceive that entity to be. User interface designers can make an online entity appear "more human" by giving it a face, gestures, a humanlike voice, conversational language, even a consistent "personality." The more realistic the interaction appears to the user, the higher their level of engagement and the more they will learn and remember from the experience (Pfeiffer et al. 2013).

Another reason for the popularity of chatbots comes from the way the technology is deployed. In the "real world," conversations take time. There is a back-and-forth cadence between the two people sharing the experience.

There are pauses while one person considers what the other has said before giving a reply.

Conversations also require context. Each party develops their next response based on what has come before. This gives you the potential to make every engagement with the chatbot unique. No two users will input exactly the same responses in the same order, so no two "conversations" will be the same.

We typically see two basic types of conversations in chatbot interactions:

Information-seeking conversations involve drilling down through a content base to deliver useful documents or links to the user. Examples of this type of conversation include content curation and customized course recommendations. A benefit of using a bot for this purpose is that it can "learn" to improve recommendations based on the responses from users. It's a perfect example of machine learning in action.

Two-way conversations can involve giving in-the-moment answers to a user in need of help on the job, such as handling objections or completing a company form. While providing instant, "in the flow of work" support, the bot is also recording the types of questions that are asked and identifies steps in the flow that appear to be causing the most difficulty (Bersin 2019). It is important to note that these conversations can take place via text (on a mobile phone or other screen) or as a one- or even two-way voice conversation. NLP allows users to simply speak into a microphone; the machine interprets that speech input, and replies either via text or via robotically generated speech.

Today, the chatbot is the preferred online interface for most users. While early attempts to create a machine that spoke to humans were usually clunky and frustrating (at least for the humans), the chatbot has become widely accepted, particularly when the user is looking for a quick response or support outside of regular business hours (Baer 2018). The most popular uses of a chatbot based on a 2018 study (Devaney 2018) are:

- getting a quick answer in an emergency (37 percent)
- resolving a complaint or problem (35 percent)
- getting detailed answers or explanations (35 percent)
- finding a human customer service assistant (34 percent)
- making a reservation (e.g., restaurant or hotel) (33 percent)
- paying a bill (29 percent)
- buying a basic item (27 percent)

- getting ideas and inspiration for purchases (22 percent)
- communicating with multiple brands using one program (18 percent)
- none of these things (15 percent)
- buying an expensive item (13 percent).

How to Use a Chatbot in Your Education or Training Program

If the talent development profession follows the trends exhibited in other businesses, we can expect chatbots to become the preferred means of interacting with learning technology in the near future (Srdanovic 2018).

So far, we've discussed the use case of chatbots for consumer interactions, because that was a starting point for the technology. Note that engaging with a chatbot is slower than other forms of human-to-computer interfaces. If we think about learning as a consumer-driven activity, then we can find many ways to make the case that chatbots develop talent and deliver learning experiences, including the following.

Interview Learners to Customize the Curriculum

A chatbot can function very much like a trusted advisor, asking the right questions to help the learner clarify their interests and point them toward appropriate training or courses. For example, a chatbot might help a college student choose a major, or recommend an appropriate certification to an IT tech. If connected to a learning performance system, the bot might use individual or team performance data to recommend training to close performance gaps or take performance to the next level.

Deliver Performance Support at the Time of Need

When a worker is on a manufacturing floor, or a salesperson is meeting with a customer, there's no time to fire up a laptop and search for a solution to a problem. But they might be able to ask a question on their smartphone and receive targeted advice, right when they need it most. One of my clients is embedding intelligent chatbots into online reference documents and order-processing tools. The bot offers suggestions and help whenever the user appears to be "stuck," or searching for the next step.

Challenge the Learner to Reflect

In today's fast-paced digital environment, there is often little, if any, time allowed for reflection. Yet, as educator John Dewey said, "We learn from reflecting on experience" (Rodgers 2002). The conversational nature of the chatbot can bring back reflection, by asking questions that require a deeper response than simply choosing the most likely option from a multiple-choice question.

Imagine a new manager, struggling with the difficult decision of whether an employee should be fired. With access to company policies and employee records, the chatbot could ask the right questions, based on legal constraints and corporate policy, to help the manager make an informed decision. The bot can take the manager through a decision tree, to determine if firing is the only option left to address the issue. Along the way, the manager may find other ways to address the issue. Perhaps the employee needs training, or an issue at home is distracting the employee and affecting their performance. Notice that the use of AI to stimulate reflection doesn't require the program to make the decision. It simply serves as a sounding board for the human user.

At some point, a meeting with a human expert in HR may be necessary. The bot can recommend this option and help schedule an appointment. When the meeting takes place with the HR professional, the manager will have their preliminary thoughts and documentation organized, based on the recommendations made by the bot.

Provide 24/7 Performance Coaching
In today's world of work, the employee may need support at any time, anywhere in the world. Access to a chatbot can provide much-needed coaching and support in a wide variety of applications.

New Employee Onboarding Bot
One of my clients uses an HR onboarding bot on the landing page of the company intranet. After the user has been online a few seconds, the bot appears and offers to help. The bot is linked to the personnel database, so it is able to address the employee by name: "Hello, Sue, how can I help you today?" While available to all employees, it is specifically designed to support the needs of new employees, who must navigate a complicated list of tasks and training to begin their new role in a complex global organization.

Sales Coach Bot

The sales coach chatbot has been built to provide sales professionals with realistic practice in handling customer objections. The more the bot is used, the more nuanced the responses from the "customer" become. The bot has been programmed to react negatively when the sales professional uses ineffective or unprofessional techniques to try to manipulate the customer into a decision. It responds positively when the correct sales approach has been applied.

New Manager Bot

This bot is designed to support employees who are making the transition from serving as a top performer in their current job to their first supervisor or manager role. New managers must acquire a whole new skill set on the fly, often without the benefit of formal training. This bot provides in-the-moment support for management tasks, such as payroll, attendance, expense management, performance reviews, handling difficult employees, recruiting, hiring, and many other tasks that can be challenging for a new manager.

Direct User Attention Where It Needs to Be

The harsh reality of digital media is that most people don't read it. They scroll and skim, often not even doing that all the way to the end of the page or document. If you have important content posted online, a chatbot can help direct learner attention where it needs to be, by sharing links and asking pointed questions. For example, a single "Hi there. Did you notice the announcement at the top of the page?" can go a lot further than sending out a message from management that begins with "Please read" (Manjoo 2013).

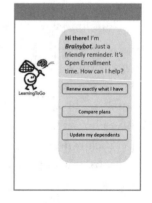

In this example, the user is invited to tell the chatbot what they need to do. The ongoing "conversation" allows the program to get more and more specific before making a recommendation.

Assess Knowledge and Retention

According to the U.S. Department of Education, assessments should be learning experiences (Kelly 2016). However, the typical standardized test is at best a poor instrument for achieving this end. Because a chatbot can be programmed to deliver questions in an order that responds to the learner's previous answers, we can use chatbot technology to simulate the Socratic method for asking questions, turning an assessment from a "gotcha" moment to one of insight and discovery. I developed this example to help high-

school students demonstrate their scientific understanding of the challenges faced by the endangered honeybee population.

Curate Content

According to Forbes, 2.5 quintillion bytes of data are created each day at our current pace (March 2018). As available digital information continues to explode, content curation becomes more and more important to the learning profession. An intelligent bot can use the keywords entered by the user to search for relevant, credible information and deliver suggestions. Remember, the conversational tone of the interface makes it far more likely that the user will accept and act on the recommendation. A well-designed chatbot feels like a friendly advisor.

In this example, the bot identifies the needs of the user, recommends appropriate content, and checks that recommendation by asking for feedback.

Collect and Analyze Learner Feedback and Behavioral Data

Perhaps the most valuable use of chatbots is one that most users don't even think about. While the user is interacting with the bot, the program is collecting all sorts of data on that user. Information such as how often and how long an individual engages with the bot, what links they click or don't click, and what questions they ask are all easily captured and converted into meaningful insights by the underlying AI. This steady stream of data can be used to improve the learner experience, identify new topics or questions, and recognize trends in user preferences and desires. Even the simplest chatbot application has the ability to develop powerful insights from the user data collected on your intranet, webpage, or LMS. I've posted a few examples and worksheets in the Resource Guide to give you some ideas.

Remember to Build in Behavior Change

You may have noticed a secondary effect that is achieved from deploying each of the previous examples. In addition to solving an immediate need, they teach users how to self-serve the next time the same issue or question occurs. A well-designed bot should always provide links or suggestions for where to go for help the next time: "For future reference. . . ." This approach makes your chatbot an education and change management tool, as well as a coach and guide.

Chatbots Are a Slower Interface

A common misconception is that chatbots make the user experience more efficient. In fact, the chatbot interface is intended to take time, to give the user the opportunity to reflect and interact with the bot in a manner that is more satisfying than simply checking boxes on a form. This "slowness" makes it a perfect tool for enhancing learning, because it gives us a digital experience that we can use to slow down the learning process—at least long enough to let the learner reflect and formulate a question.

Build It or Buy It?

A classic question when acquiring any new technology is whether you should build it using in-house resources or pay an outside firm to build it for you. I can't answer that question for you, but I can tell you this—you should follow the same process, regardless of your decision. In the back of the book and on the Resource Site, I've included a few tools to help you:

Build It or Buy It? This form allows you to answer a few pertinent questions to determine if it makes more sense for you to build the bot yourself or hire an outside firm to do it for you.

How to Choose a Supplier: If you decide that you want to use an outside provider, this checklist will help you determine the best partner for your project.

You can even incorporate the questions into a formal request for proposal (RFP) if that is needed.

How to Manage a Technology Supplier: Even if you are "farming out" the programming to someone else, you must stay engaged throughout the process, to ensure that you get the results you need. This guide gives you a few best practices to get your relationship with your supplier off to a good start and keep it moving in a positive direction.

How to Build a Chatbot: If you're taking the "build it" route, this guide will give you several ideas.

Mobile Coach founder Vince Hahn created his first chatbot in sixth grade, and later translated his passion into a leading enterprise software as a service (SaaS) platform for designing, deploying, and managing chatbots. I met Vince at ATD TechKnowledge a couple of years ago when he attended the presentation my friend Joe Ganci and I made on using chatbots for e-learning. Vince has lots of experience deploying custom bots for educational purposes, so I asked him why chatbots are so effective for training purposes. Here's what he told me: "A chatbot can produce immediate responses in a friendly and easy-to-use conversational user interface. The scalability that chatbots offer makes it possible to handle thousands of conversations at once. Chatbots don't have to sleep and they don't get tired. Today, many organizations are deploying chatbots to help onboard, train, and assist employees and their managers. This is a prime example of matching a new AI-powered technology with a use case that has relevancy today and is well within the technology's current capabilities."

At LearningToGo, we use a guide to help clients make informed decisions about new learning technology. It may be that building in-house is your best option, but to be sure, this tool helps you evaluate the often hidden costs of building in-house. Some of these costs include lost time, lack of resources, and the cost of ongoing maintenance and user support.

You'll find resources on the build versus buy question in the Appendix and on the Resource Site.

Chapter Summary

While it may seem like a new approach to you, chatbots have been proven to support and engage users in a wide variety of other industries, so this is an AI-driven application that you can implement with a high degree of confidence and a high likelihood of success. In this chapter, I've given you a few basic considerations to get you started. However, the key to implementing chatbots—or any learning technology—is in the planning and execution. The tools in the back of the book should help you achieve your goals. We've covered a lot of ground in this chapter, but you won't really be able to apply it until you roll up your sleeves and start building. Here are a few tips to keep in mind:

- Just do one thing with your chatbot. Solve one problem and demonstrate that you've solved it. That will be more than enough.
- Constrain, constrain, constrain. Keep a laser-like focus on the problem you want to solve and how you will solve it.
- Think in terms of how your bot might extend a service you already provide, rather than deliver something brand-new.
- Build a "minimally viable product" first. You can always embellish the look and feel of the bot after you're sure that it works.
- Make it personal. The power of the chatbot lies in its ability to trick the user's brain into having an authentic experience. Make it easier for that to happen by giving your bot some personality and having a little fun.
- Test, implement, test. It's like every shampoo instruction: "Wash, rinse, repeat." It's my number-one recommendation for achieving best results.

Although highly effective as a stand-alone solution, the benefits of a chatbot can multiply when incorporated with other technologies, such as embedding a bot in more traditional e-learning programs as an alternative to branching or simulations. It can also be deployed at the front of an LMS, taking advantage of the conversation illusion to make the LMS experience more engaging and supportive for the learner. We'll talk about this and many other applications of AI that are possible with a "smart LMS" in chapter 4: "Make Your Learning Management Systems Smarter."

4

Make Your Learning Management System Smarter

The dawn is rising on another day, and everywhere you look, people are learning. Aisha works from home and is taking advantage of a quiet moment to catch up on some of her required computer security training. Her employer's learning management system (LMS) has been reminding her, in increasingly shrill tones, that this training is overdue.

"ATTENTION! YOU HAVE PAST DUE TASKS," screams the subject line, deploying the classic no-no of sending a message in all caps.

With a huge sigh, she drops what she is doing and logs in to her company LMS, hoping to escape the "naughty list," which tells managers which employees have not completed mandatory training. Like most folks, she's been putting it off because her previous experiences have all been painfully boring. But this time it's different. The training feels like it's been written just for her. It highlights security risks that are relevant to her job and presents scenarios that she faces every day. Because the content is so targeted to what she needs to know, it's also a much shorter course than Aisha expected. When the system offers her another mandatory course, she decides to take that one, too, and enjoys a similar, personalized experience.

Harold is a sailor on board the USS *Mercy*, a Navy hospital ship. When he isn't on duty, he's also a college student, taking courses online via the ship's

Wi-Fi system. His program is an "open degree," so he's able to choose from courses offered at his own school, programs provided by the Navy or other schools, and even massive open online courses (MOOCs) from providers like Coursera and Teachable. He chooses his learning experiences from a curated list that was generated by an algorithm. As he completes items on the list, the system keeps track of completions by learning outcomes, rather than course numbers or titles. He's progressing much faster toward his degree in electrical engineering with this approach, and he's excited about the new career that is waiting for him after just three more learning outcomes are satisfied.

Halfway around the world, Sanjay is reviewing the results of his latest training project. His firm has invested in a new LMS with powerful analytics tools. At first, Sanjay was excited about the power this new system offered. But now, faced with myriad charts and graphs that appear to tell him every time each learner sneezed, he's overwhelmed by the number of choices at his fingertips. How can he make sense of all this data? It will take him at least several hours to review just a single report. And how can he integrate all this information into something he can present to his boss? For a moment, he longs for the simpler days when the only reports he could run were course completions and quiz scores.

Alice is a retired systems administrator. She used to manage the IT department of a large public-school district, but she recently retired. Already comfortable with technology, she's been indulging her passion for art by visiting the great galleries of Europe online. It's all part of a course she's taking just for her own enjoyment. Today she's visiting the Louvre. Then she's playing a nice round of golf with her friends.

Dave's a deliveryman for a major online retailer. Today, he watched a demonstration of an experimental robot that can load the truck, program the self-driving vehicle to the customer's address, unload the right package, and deliver it to their front door. Then the robot took a photo of the package to verify delivery and texted the customer. Placing a call to the customer's mobile phone, the robot chirped, "Your package has arrived. Have a nice day," The bot returned to the truck, started the self-driving program, and proceeded to the next location. Most of the people in the room were enchanted by this new technology, but Dave is worried about his job. He wonders if he should enroll in that coding class his boss mentioned to him.

Why are we fascinated by the next shiny thing? If you don't have it yet, every new learning technology looks like the solution to all your problems. "If only we could have that [insert shiny new technology here], our training program would be so much more effective." It's possible that the next great thing is just around the corner and will transform our lives. But history reveals a different pattern.

"Students today can't prepare bark to calculate their problems. They depend on their slates. . . . What will they do when their slate is dropped and it breaks? They will be unable to write!"
—Teachers' Conference, 1703

"Students today depend too much upon ink. They don't know how to use a penknife to sharpen a pencil. Pen and ink will never replace the pencil."
—National Association of Teachers, 1907

"Students today depend upon store-bought ink. They don't know how to make their own. When they run out of ink they will be unable to write words or ciphers until their next trip to the settlement."
—Rural American Teacher, 1929

"Students today depend upon these expensive fountain pens. They can no longer write with a straight pen and nib (not to mention sharpening their own quills)."
—*PTA Gazette,* 1941

"Ball point pens will be the ruin of education in our country."
—Federal Teacher, 1950

"There are still many . . . who worry that the calculator use will impair students' mathematical ability and result in mathematical illiteracy."
—School Superintendents' Forum, 1997

"My mind now expects to take in information the way the Net distributes it: in a swiftly moving stream of particles. Once I was a scuba diver in the sea of words. Now I zip along the surface like a guy on a Jet Ski."
—Nicholas Carr, "Is Google Making Us Stupid?," 2008

If we don't have the technology yet, we assume it will cure all our ills. If we have it, we see it as the source of all our troubles. Either way, we tend to assume that the technology itself is responsible for learning, losing sight of the fact that meaning is constructed in the brain of each learner. As Shakespeare's Hamlet says, "There is nothing either good or bad, but thinking makes it so."

In this chapter, we focus on how AI can enhance our human capital systems to support the learning process. It's important to remember as we go through this chapter that these systems do not produce the learning experience itself. That's created in the mind of the learners, one brain at a time.

Netflix Your Learning

The amount of data produced every single day continues to grow exponentially. In 2017, human beings generated 2.5 quintillion bytes of data a day—that's 18 zeroes! As talent development professionals, how can we maintain high levels of performance in a time of unrelenting change? The solution is often called "lifelong learning," but implementing it isn't quite as simple as it seems. The learning profession is no longer about "checking the boxes" to satisfy some government or management requirements. It's about applying science to transform the way people live their lives. When we do that successfully, the organization and society at large flourish. This sounds great, but how do you make it happen? One approach is a massive experiment that combines neuroscience, data analytics, and machine learning; there's a good chance you're already a willing subject.

Here's how it works.

It starts with your brain. We have the brain we have for one reason—it keeps us alive. Our brain, along with the rest of our body, evolved to do one thing—preserve our species. One of the strongest survival traits we have is our desire to learn; we are fascinated by the new. We're infatuated with puzzles, games, mysteries, and contests. When we figure something out, our brain gives us a powerful reward. It releases the chemical dopamine, which makes us feel great. When something feels great, like eating, exercising, or having sex, we tend to find opportunities to do that again. This chemical is so powerful that it can make you addicted. Once you get a taste, you're always hungry for more.

Your brain uses the reward cycle to encourage you to perform lifesaving behaviors. One of those behaviors is learning, and we're all addicted to it. In

The Selfish Gene, Richard Dawkins sheds light on how the human brain evolved to be such a relentlessly effective survival machine, and how this single trait has so profoundly shaped our species.

Now gather a ton of data from a ton of brains. Netflix has more than 100 million subscribers and tracks these subscribers down to very specific behaviors (McFadden 2019). They know a lot about you: When you watch TV, what programs you watch, who else is in your family and what they watch, how you rate what you've watched, what you watch straight through and what you don't finish, which titles you binge by watching multiple episodes in a row, what episodes you watch over and over again, and more. With the average American watching more than four hours of television a day, that's a lot of data.

Set a machine loose on the data. If we had to analyze all that information with our brains alone, it would take years to recognize the patterns in just a small sample. Here's where machine learning comes in handy. Algorithms are programs that tell a computer how to perform a task, such as recognize patterns and make predictions. These algorithms can often see patterns that would not be intuitive to even the most gifted human analyst.

Netflix uses data analytics algorithms to see patterns in individual users to make personalized recommendations. Then they connect those recommendations to users who have similar patterns to create new collections and categories that can be very specific. The prediction algorithm can also tell Netflix how their audience will respond to programming, such as which programs are likely to go viral within the first few minutes of viewing, and which programs are going to find a small but fiercely loyal, cult-like following. They're using what we know about neuroscience to predict what sort of experiences will trigger the dopamine effect for each individual, and they have an algorithm to find the programming that triggers this response most effectively. Every time you select a program that Netflix recommends for you, you're teaching the algorithm more about yourself, your preferences, and how you interact with and consume their content. They don't have to attach a scanning device to your head to see the addictive rush you get from an absorbing online experience; your behavior gives you away every time. Each time the algorithm is used, it gets better at doing its job, so the predictions get better and better. The approach is called contextuality, and it creates the illusion of mass marketing content that feels uniquely selected to appeal to each individual customer because, behind the scenes, it actually was.

Sprinkle with social learning. Another trait that is hardwired into our DNA as a species is our need to learn from one another. *Psychology Today* magazine puts it simply: "People learn by watching other people." Netflix and many other online marketers use this tendency to teach us which products, books, or programs to purchase by showing us the behavior of others. When we read a review on Yelp or check the number of "stars" before we make our selection, we're letting the behavior of others help us make a decision. These "recommender systems" combine your own behavior (such as how you rated a similar program) with the behaviors of many other users, then filter for similarities between users so that in fact you are making recommendations to yourself.

Apply broadly and stir often. Of course, Netflix isn't the only company that is deploying this approach to create a customized consumer experience on a massive scale. Amazon uses a predictive application that anticipates which products will be ordered a day before customers have even placed their orders, so that warehouses and distribution points can have the right supply of the right things to meet anticipated needs (Selyukh 2018). Google uses information from humans and machines to predict traffic congestion for Google Maps, and uses similar algorithms to predict your search terms before you've finished typing (Johnson 2019). The U.S. government uses AI to make predictions about enemy troop movements (Olckers 2020). NASA uses AI to predict when an astronaut is about to suffer too much fatigue to reliably pilot a spaceship (Shekhtman 2019). (All these examples rely on data sets of quality, reliable information. And lots of it.)

Apply AI to Analyze Big Data and Gain Big Insights

The fields of analytics and AI have evolved along convergent paths. About 30 years ago, business analytics consisted primarily of gathering and summarizing data. As analysis methods became more sophisticated, more specific business intelligence techniques allowed insights, predictions, and recommendations to be generated from the data collected. A few years later, data mining techniques were developed to automate the work of analyzing very large data sets—big data—to discover patterns that could predict the outcomes of business decisions. Most recently, the use of machine learning, AI, and other advances have allowed us to use intelligent machines to perform analytics without human direction.

AI and data analytics can be understood as a layered system, like the layers of an onion, with each successive layer becoming more and more complex. These layers include rule-based automated systems, machine learning, and deep learning.

Let's peel back the onion one layer at a time.

Rule-based automation. A rule-based system allows us to build automation by leveraging domain-based knowledge. For example, we can use data on how humans process routine customer requests to automate the process using a text-based chatbot.

The automation works through explicit programming—if X happens, do Y. It relies on a huge database of domain knowledge, such as policies and procedures, and queries the data using keywords to determine the right course of action in a given situation.

Machine learning. As we've seen, machine learning is a subfield of AI that focuses on the ability to train a model to understand and predict the value of some quantity of new data for which the target value or classification is unknown.

Rather than tell the program how to do this, we allow it to learn from experience, by following the standards we set forth in the initial program. Then we let it continue to learn.

When we say "without intervention," that's not entirely true. The intervention takes place at the start of the process, when the rules are written that determine how the machine will learn. Human programmers write these rules. They tell the program how to sift through information—the source of the machine's learning experience—to achieve certain goals, and what sources of information to use. Then they expose the program to huge amounts of data, and the learning begins. Let's say you want to develop a program that can recognize cancer cells in magnetic resonance imaging (MRI) scans. The initial rules will describe how to identify a cancerous cell, along with numerous examples. Then we begin to expose the machine to scans without specifying the result. As the machine applies the rules, it receives feedback, whether its answers are correct or incorrect. It doesn't take long for the machine to develop almost perfect performance. Now it's time to subject the machine to raw data, for which the result is not yet known. Humans will continue to spot-check the results as quality assurance, but the machine now performs much faster and far more accurately than its human designers, so it increasingly becomes the standard for this type of analysis. Sound too futuristic to be true? It happened in 2019. What data-analysis needs does your organization face? You may be able to apply machine learning to gain new insights (Thomson 2020).

Although most corporate training departments and educational institutions are still on the fence about AI, China has jumped in with enthusiasm and is putting billions of dollars into what it calls "intelligent education" (Chawla 2019).

The initiative focuses on replacing or supplementing human teachers with robotic instructors that adapt to each student to provide personalized learning experiences. Some solutions use student performance to adjust the curriculum to an individual's strengths and weaknesses, while others use biometric information, such facial expressions and voice inflection, to determine a student's level of understanding and engagement with a virtual instructor.

Because of the large numbers involved, these programs are making great strides in the development of educational AI very quickly. Artificial intelligence systems require massive data sets in order to "learn" through experience with their human users. In 2017, one startup operating in China boasted more than 1 million users, who were working with the program five days a week, for the entire school day. That's a lot of data, and a lot of potential machine learning.

In India, another market with access to massive numbers of students, the focus is also on using AI to replace the instructor in the classroom. In 2019 about 200 companies were providing AI solutions to deliver content and adjust the learning experience to individual performance (Tracxn 2019).

If you are working in corporate training, human resources, talent development, or any level of education, chances are you will be working with some version of intelligent artificial teachers or coaches in the very near future.

Deep learning. At the heart of the onion is deep learning (Figure 4-1). Deep learning is a complex branch of machine learning that uses neural networks designed to mimic the human brain, performing highly complex tasks with greater accuracy than other systems—and sometimes even humans—can produce. Because it is not given a pattern as a starting point, deep learning is capable of finding patterns and insights that would not be possible for machine learning or human analysis alone. These new insights are particularly valuable for predicting human behavior, which is where we come in (Dickson 2019).

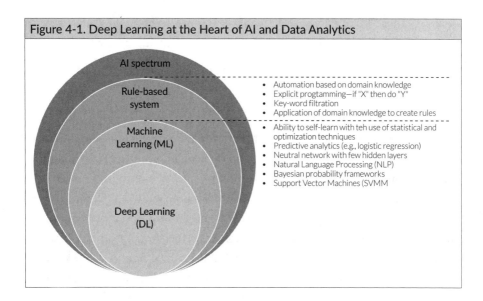

Figure 4-1. Deep Learning at the Heart of AI and Data Analytics

AI spectrum

Rule-based system
- Automation based on domain knowledge
- Explicit progtamming—if "X" then do "Y"
- Key-word filtration
- Application of domain knowledge to create rules

Machine Learning (ML)
- Ability to self-learn with teh use of statistical and optimization techniques
- Predictive analytics (e.g., logistic regression)
- Neutral network with few hidden layers
- Natural Language Processing (NLP)
- Bayesian probability frameworks
- Support Vector Machines (SVMM)

Deep Learning (DL)

What Is Big Data?

Data can mean just about anything that is created and shared. Consider your own experience. In a single hour, you might read an email on your PC, send a text on your phone, download a podcast, watch a video, and post a tweet. Each of these examples is a different type of data and requires different strategies for capture and analysis. And these are only a few examples of the diversity of data available online today. Big data doesn't even have to be online. It can exist on secure servers or massive paper-based files that have been digitized.

Big data refers to data sets that are so voluminous and complex that traditional data-processing software is inadequate to deal with them. When organizations try to deal with these massive data sets, they often run into challenges, because we humans are just not built to handle the massive amount of information that we generate today. Big data has four dimensions, known as volume, variety, velocity, and veracity.

Volume

Volume refers to the staggering amount of information that must be present to qualify as "big." The more data you can feed your algorithm, the deeper it learns and the more efficient and accurate it can become in predicting user behavior. Network behemoths like Google, Amazon, Netflix, and others are pulling data from billions or trillions of records from sources like websites, customer support centers, chatbots, social media, and e-commerce systems to generate these huge data sets. How big is big in this context? Data scientists work with petabytes (1,024 terabytes) or exabytes (1,024 petabytes) in applications like this.

Variety

Another characteristic of big data that makes it an interesting challenge for AI is the combination of different types of information in the same set, requiring a lot of processing power and understanding to interpret it. For example, a human being might be able to correlate information from when trains arrive at the station and how many passengers get off, but if we wanted to factor in weather, track conditions, and days of the week, we'd end up with a pretty unwieldy spreadsheet. Traditional data analysis tends to focus on information that is discrete—it is bounded by very specific rules that can be fit into a simple framework. We call this "structured data." Test scores, completion rates, and course registrations fit into this category.

By contrast, unstructured data doesn't have a predictable set of rules. It could be a profile image of an employee, a verbatim comment about a course, or the biometric track a learner's eyes follow as they study a screen in an e-learning course.

The combination of unstructured and structured data in the same analysis is what makes up the variety characteristic of big data.

Velocity

Data is coming at us from all directions, and it is coming faster every day. To benefit from big data insights, companies must be able to capture, analyze, and use this massive amount of information as quickly as it is coming in. Human beings alone could never keep up with this "fire hose" of information, so big-data solutions must include strategies to control and keep up with the speed of incoming data. These strategies employ artificial intelligence to process the flood of information almost as quickly as it is coming in. If the information isn't coming at a feverish velocity, chances are it isn't really a big data application.

Veracity

Data must also be accurate if our AI program is to produce useful insights. The degree of uncertainty will reflect the veracity (or lack of it) of the data. It's a simple concept that is often summarized as GIGO in the IT world. "Garbage in, garbage out" applies to computer programming, data analytics, and education. It's all about making quality inputs to achieve a quality result.

What Problem Are You Trying to Solve? Is AI the Answer?

It is important to remember that big data, AI, and other analytics capabilities are most useful when traditional analytics systems and software cannot adequately solve the problem. Big data does not replace traditional analytics (plain old number-crunching by human beings with spreadsheets)—both have different uses, depending on the problem you are trying to solve.

Until you find a significant problem to solve—one that is keeping folks in the C-suite up at night—you're unlikely to get the funding and sponsorship to move forward with an AI initiative.

Don't have that large a data set? You still have options. There are several tools available that tap into larger data sets and allow you to tailor reports to your needs. A list of resources to get you started is in the resources section of the Appendix.

Can your organization use the same approach to make predictions about LMS searches or learner course completion? That depends. It takes a lot of data to train a predictive algorithm, so this technology is usually seen in large organizations with tons of data points. (Hence the usage by Netflix, Amazon, and Google.) If you're fortunate enough to work in a large organization, they are likely already using predictive analytics and machine learning to develop new products, make wise investments, provide customer support, and protect their systems against cyberattacks. Your talent development team may be able to tap into data scientists and AI developers in your organization to design an algorithm for your organization.

Or, you could just buy a smart LMS.

Can an LMS Be Smart?

In 2017, I wrote an article for ATD's *TD* magazine, "The Near Future of Learning Automation: The Smart LMS." Early iterations of the learning management system first started appearing in the 1970s to support a truly disruptive innovation that we now call "e-learning." Since then, these two learning tools have grown up together, each evolving as the other pushed the envelope a bit further, creating an iterative path to innovation. As LMS technology made things easier to do, instructional designers found ways to use its features to enhance the learning experience. When instructional designers demanded more of the LMS, providers found a way to deliver better video support, new ways of tracking learning experiences, and a wider array of features to engage learners. Yet most of my clients tell me that their relationship with their LMS has been producing diminishing returns for years.

However, many modern LMS systems combine data analytics and AI/ machine learning to do a lot more than spit out completion reports and Level 1 learner reaction survey results (Kirkpatrick and Kirkpatrick 2016). Today's "smart LMS" is programmed to "learn" the skills that each individual employee needs to meet business goals. Algorithms tell the LMS computer code how to determine which skills are required, based on business objectives. The LMS then produces a customized learning plan for each employee based on gaps indicated by skill assessment results. No more writing assessments; you simply upload your existing content, and the system writes the questions. As business goals change, the LMS, guided by the underlying algorithms, adjusts immediately and changes learning plans as needed to fill the newly identified skills gaps. This new type of LMS has become possible only with the advent of machine learning. The algorithm provides detailed instructions that allow the LMS to discover the needs of the business and each individual in your organization. No matter how much things change, the system will continue to adjust learning plans automatically, responding to updating company objectives. Instead of trying to plan for every possibility, the "machine"—in this case, the LMS—"learns" what is needed by analyzing the data according to the instructions contained in the algorithm. You'll find more tools for selecting and deploying these features in your LMS on the Resource Site.

The Virtuous Cycle of Data and AI

A virtuous cycle is a practice or process that is improved by its results. The smart LMS can deliver a virtuous cycle of continuous performance improvement by continually responding to learner needs based on performance. The more deeply you can connect the LMS to performance data and real-time support information, the stronger this virtuous cycle can become.

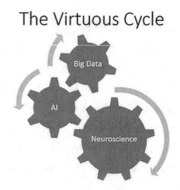

The Virtuous Cycle

Reap the Benefits of the Smart LMS

We may eventually develop an even longer list of benefits for learning automation as we gain more experience with this new technology. For now, here are the top advantages I see for early adopters:

Shortened needs analysis process. The smart LMS will be able to help you conduct a needs analysis by delivering assessments based on existing content. If the employee doesn't pass the assessment, and the skill is flagged for their current or future role, the LMS will add that training to the learning plan. Detailed reports can show you a snapshot of needed skills versus assessment scores for your entire organization, group, or individual. You should be able to spend less time on analysis and more time on developing content and robust learning experiences.

Making assessments part of the learning process instead of just checking a box. According to the U.S. Department of Education, assessments should be learning experiences. However, the typical standardized test is a poor instrument for achieving this end. The standardized multiple-choice test has its place in training and education, but it doesn't really measure what society thinks it measures. A multiple-choice question measures how well the learner can guess at the answer by eliminating incorrect options and then choosing the most likely answer from the list of remaining choices. (Many machine learning programs operate the same way.)

While this is certainly a valuable work and life skill (suppose you have to choose something to eat for lunch from a menu of items you don't usually eat), it isn't a measure of how much you've learned. Because learning results in changing behavior, the only way to truly measure if someone has learned is to evaluate their behavior under a controlled set of constraints. If someone has already demonstrated mastery of a particular skill in previous lessons, for example, there is no need to have them repeat that performance on the final exam.

In today's digital era, recall is often no longer a relevant requirement for education and training. Nearly everything we need to "know" can be found online. What we need to be able to do is apply that information effectively on the job or in school. By tracking where an individual is struggling, the system can provide targeted review content and continually measure improvement, linking the learning experience to on-the-job performance. An LMS empowered with artificial intelligence can become the perfect teacher, always ready with a new tip or a challenging question.

For example, Pearson, the textbook publisher, has an AI-driven English-language assessment tool (English Benchmark) that can use a student's spoken or written input to:

- Assess where the student is in their development.
- Identify gaps in their knowledge.
- Select learning activities to close those gaps.
- Reassess on a continuous basis to fine-tune the learning.

The product is aligned with the Global Scale of English (GSE) and the Common European Framework of Reference for Languages (CEFR) and uses an algorithm to adapt to the needs of each individual learner. The algorithm uses a specialized type of natural language processing called latent semantic analysis, which can analyze and score writing based on the meaning behind words—and not just their superficial characteristics. This approach helps us determine how well the student recognizes the contextual meaning of words, which vary depending on the rest of the words in the sentence.

While the Pearson tool is focused on one particular subject, the assessment-learning-assessment cycle could be applied to any academic subject or job competency.

When businesses and schools all over the world closed as part of the effort to slow the spread of the coronavirus, we experienced firsthand the need for a nimble response to unexpected changes that affect the learning process. On a smaller scale, these pivots are happening all the time, and a smart LMS can help you meet those demands. For example, if your company decides that your customer care team needs to start making sales during inbound calls, you need to be able to update the program to address the new skills required to assess, teach, and support those goals.

We've been talking about personalized learning for decades, and the technology has finally caught up. Because no two people are alike, no two employees will have exactly the same learning plan, even if they are serving in the same role.

When employees receive learning suggestions that are truly customized to them, they will probably respond with more excitement about their work and a greater appreciation for the company that has invested so sincerely in their future. While this new type of LMS will likely appeal to all learners, Millennials are already demanding this sort of customized approach, which mirrors their experience as consumers.

Buy a Smart LMS Smartly

Learning management systems don't come cheap, so this is an AI-enabled technology that may take some time to acquire. Like any other major purchase, start by defining your goals, then look for a platform that supports those goals most effectively. Only you can decide what you want in a smart LMS, but here's what training managers said they're looking for, according to a recent survey by LMS provider Docebo:

- data analytics (50 percent)
- social/collaborative tools (44 percent)
- mobile delivery (43 percent)
- content management (37 percent)
- virtual classrooms (35 percent).

Plan for Your Next LMS Now

We can teach calculus, music, marketing, French, or anything else using any type of technology. We could even just talk about the subject. Marshall McLuhan is famous for saying "The medium is the message," in reference to what was then the new entertainment medium of television. But when I try to extrapolate that concept to today's breathless excitement about learning technologies, it feels empty. Is Twitter the message? Facebook? YouTube? If we're able to do anything at all, we learning professionals can help an individual find their own way toward meaning. We don't need the latest and greatest of anything to make that happen. The key is to start by using the tools at hand. And when better tools become available, use those, too. No shiny new tool is going to do the hard work for us, so having an out-of-date LMS is no excuse for delivering an antiquated learning experience. Conversely, buying a new shiny thing won't absolve us of our responsibility to apply what we know to create an exciting, engaging, supportive approach that provides a personalized journey for each learner.

Two things are highly likely at this moment:

- Your current LMS is at least a bit outdated.
- You have a new LMS somewhere in your future.

Look for These Features in Your Next LMS

As described in the 1950s by the father of modern computer science, Alan Turing, "What we want is a machine that can learn from experience" (Turing 1950). This description fits the concept of a smart LMS very well. With each learner, the smart LMS should be able to get better at making personalized recommendations, linking learning experience to key performance indicators (KPIs), and delivering assessments that measure the learner's ability to do their job, rather just measuring their success in multiple-choice tests. In an article for *HR Technologist,* researcher Annabelle Smyth summarized several key benefits to gain from an AI-enabled LMS.

Smart Curation

With AI in the mix, e-learning platforms can offer smart curation and personalization features, which will enable learners to study at their own pace and in the style that suits them. Using predictive modeling, AI can create anticipated learning paths by monitoring a learner's performance and adjust the path so that it never becomes too daunting or too slow for immersion to take place (the "Goldilocks Zone") (Dawson 2019).

Likewise, AI can suggest which lessons to take next and how frequent testing should be, and offer guidance in terms of which courses the learner should tackle to achieve the next level of performance. This level of personalization will allow e-learning platforms to rise above the competition and ensure that individuals are satisfied with the amount of information and skills they've accumulated from using them.

In 2020, I asked a design analyst for the learning consulting firm Aptara to summarize what trends they are seeing with their clients. Here's what I learned. "Organizations are adopting platforms that use AI to customize content for specific learner needs. These same systems also use machine learning by mining the data generated by learners using the system to customize learning experiences. As learning grows beyond knowledge silos, and the knowledge acquisition required is by nature cross-functional, such systems will deliver the knowledge required to the learners."

In a research report, the Association for Talent Development makes this recommendation:

> "Review features that support personalization and enable adaptation when evaluating new products or upgrades to existing systems" (ATD Research 2018).

Conversational Interface

As with other AI applications, the use of natural language programming allows the learner experience to be more engaging and personalized. For example, a digital voice assistant similar to Alexa and Siri can create a completely different experience from typing keywords into a search window to find appropriate learning experiences (see chapter 3).

Linking Performance Support

Sometimes you can't wait for the learner to make incremental improvements—you need them to perform correctly on the job. If I have a new technician in the field, I don't want them to learn through trial and error while they make mistakes with my customers. A performance support module can deliver just-in-time support, from simple tips to detailed, step-by-step instructions. The data captured during actual on-the-job performance can then be used to suggest remedial training that can be consumed at a more convenient time.

One of my clients uses an augmented reality overlay that tracks how the user is moving through the system and provides tips for those areas where the user appears to be hesitating or struggling. The system can even offer to "walk through" the process, delivering step-by-step instructions until the learner demonstrates the confidence to work on their own. The key is to avoid slowing down employees who are already competent in the skill while providing support for those who need it, so the algorithm learns how to recognize individual users and match their performance against the pattern of highly skilled users, identifying where these individuals will need additional help. With new employees, the machine might be in almost constant communication, avoiding errors and reinforcing key steps and tips. Over time, as the employee gains more confidence, these tips become fewer, coming up only occasionally.

Using AI in the Recruiting Process

So far, we've talked about what AI can do to support your employees once they are through the door. The truth is, AI's influence begins long before that first day on the job. One of the earliest applications for AI and machine learning has been in the recruiting process, and it's getting better all the time. Today most jobseekers post their résumés and other personal details online and subscribe to various social media tools to help them apply to hot jobs as they appear. What they may not realize is that employers are using these same tools to find them—or eliminate them from consideration. Large companies can use AI in a number of ways to sift through available candidates and come up with a small list of finalists for serious consideration. Jobseekers and resumes that don't make the cut never connect with a human being; the decision to move on to someone else has already been made by an algorithm. Here are a few applications that have already made their way into the workplace:

Find Qualified Candidates and Get Them Interested in Your Company

An AI application can be trained to sift through all the resumes online to find the skills and experiences that represent likely success on the job. That's the easy part, and AI has been doing the heavy lifting for this part of the process for years. The latest innovation reaches out to the candidates through email or social media and engages them. In many cases, a top candidate will receive inviting emails or social media messages before they have even considered working for a particular company. They will be wooed by an AI. And based on the rich amount of information available on each of us online, the AI has plenty of material to use to weave a cohesive campaign that feels customized to the individual candidate, because it is.

The process can also be extremely efficient, sifting through thousands of candidates to find the few who are the best fit for the job. In fact, that very speed can be a challenge sometimes. One hiring company that deployed an AI-enabled program to identify key candidates had to build some delay into the process. It seems that candidates were getting responses from the system so quickly that they didn't trust the results and questioned the validity of the system (McIlvaine 2020).

Re-engage Previous Candidates

Sometimes an applicant doesn't work out for a particular job. Even though they didn't make the final cut, these people are often highly qualified, and they already expressed an interest in the company. While a human recruiter might lose track of these individuals, a machine never forgets. AI programs can stay in touch with candidates who were turned down. Through a process called "talent rediscovery," the system automatically matches new opportunities to everyone in the database and keeps track of updated skills, all running in the background without an interruption. When the right match comes along, the candidate receives an invitation to apply. It's rewarding to the individual, who feels valued and respected by the potential employer, and it saves a lot of time and effort not having to vet a completely new person in the pipeline.

Match Candidates to the Right Jobs

I once got a call from a recruiter for a job I didn't apply for. It seems that I had applied for a job that wasn't such a good fit for my skills, but the recruiter had something else that was right up my alley. I was lucky that this human being saw my untapped potential at the time. Now that same recognition might be driven by the pattern recognition of an AI, matching candidates to potential jobs, regardless of what they originally applied for. In these instances, our machines sometimes know us better than we know ourselves.

Reimagine the Pre-employment Assessment

Many employers are using pre-employment screening, such as aptitude tests, to help narrow the field. To appeal to younger candidates, many of these screening activities are presented as games or social media "communities" that encourage participants to learn more about the company and engage with existing employees and fellow applicants. While these pre-employment activities are delivering on their promise, they are also beginning the evaluation process. Applicants will reveal a great deal about themselves and their communication skills, problem-solving approach, technical aptitude, and social skills in these activities, and all of this information produces additional data for the AI to use in the evaluation process.

Hiring organizations need to be wary of legal considerations that may put them at risk for litigation, fines, or prosecution. In the United States, for example, Title I of the Americans With Disabilities Act (ADA) makes it illegal for employers to use employment-screening tests that discriminate against qualified applicants based on their mental or physical disabilities.

Train Your Dragon Carefully

You might be surprised to see training as an AI-related term. In this context, it refers to the preliminary process of machine learning, during which the system is exposed to a wide range of variables to discover the standards and patterns it will use to make predictions and recommend actions. The AI then uses this model to make predictions based on new information that it encounters. In layman's terms, the system teaches itself and then applies what it has learned to the environment, continuously modifying the model as it goes. (Sound familiar? "Reward learning" is a concept borrowed from cognitive psychology and applied to the learning process of a neural network made of silicon, instead of carbon.)

In a famous example of (presumably) unintended consequences of machine learning, Microsoft introduced the chatbot Tay on Twitter in 2016. Within 24 hours, the AI had learned how to spew some of the most vile, racist, misogynistic language imaginable and had to be put down. The reason for the failure can be found in the way we train AIs—on huge data sets. Tay was simply put online and programmed to "listen and respond" to what was being posted online (Vincent 2016).

I'm reminded of the film *How to Train Your Dragon*:

> "Dragons can't change who they are. But who would want them to? Dragons are powerful, amazing creatures. . . . Most people . . . would say life here is better since we made peace with them. Unfortunately, dragons are still, well, dragons."

The LMS Is Not the Learning

The brain is constantly rewiring itself in response to changes detected in our environment. This remarkable capability, called neuroplasticity, tells us two important things.

First, behavior change is always possible. In fact, it is nearly unavoidable, given the onslaught of information rushing into our brains through our senses.

Second, as talent development professionals, we don't actually produce learning. We give people the framework and opportunity to learn, but they do the learning all by themselves. That's because each brain is unique—shaped by a constant stream of unique experiences and conscious choices of what to pay attention to and what to ignore or treat as background noise.

Sounds simple, doesn't it? But consider this: Every single behavior, pattern, belief, habit, superstition, bias, or preference that contributes to the person you know as you is a result of your unique experience. You have been building your own neural connections since before you were born, and you continue to tinker with your completely unique creation every single minute of your life—even when you are asleep.

The hard truth is that no training program or LMS changes behavior. I'll say that again, because you might not believe me. No course, training program, or LMS has ever changed behavior. That's because we training professionals don't own the learning process; our learners do. We can set up a situation in which people are more likely to choose to change behavior, but only the learner can actually make the choice to change, and then take the steps to put that change into effect. So the real question is, "How can we set the stage for behavior change?" Technology can help, but it can't make it happen.

I've provided a few tools in the back of the book and the Resource Site to help you make the most of your learning technology, but the learning process itself is between you and each individual you serve as a learning professional. The resources you'll find include:

- **Build It or Buy It?**
- **Do You Really Need an LMS?** A job aid with a few questions you should ask before you invest in an LMS at all.

Chapter Summary

This chapter focused on pairing AI with a familiar tool for delivering and measuring training, the learning management system. This chapter provided:

- tips on how to make your learning content "binge worthy" using the AI-driven techniques employed by Netflix, Amazon, Google, and other organizations that have become experts at personalizing the customer experience
- a look at the levels of AI, from rule-based automation to deep learning
- an overview of the four dimensions of big data and how it provides the necessary framework for machine learning
- the characteristics of an AI-enabled "smart LMS" and how to buy one
- a word of caution about the limits of what any technology can do to support the learning process.

You'll also find a list of tools in the back of the book and on the Resource Site.

Technology has come a long way in our profession, and AI promises to take it even further very quickly. With that speed comes a terrible responsibility that we need to discuss: How can we control this stunning new technology, and make sure that we're doing the right thing? That's exactly the question we address in chapter 5: "Do the Right Thing."

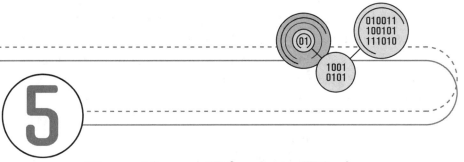

Do the Right Thing

"Technology is nothing. What's important is that you have faith in people, that they're basically good and smart, and if you give them tools, they'll do wonderful things with them." —Steve Jobs

Sampath is a philosophy major. He's writing his thesis on business ethics and faces lots of ribbing from his fellow students for writing about a subject they say is an oxymoron. But Sampath is determined to change the world. He believes that there can be such a thing as ethical behavior in a business setting, even when the players are supposed to be driven by profit and self-interest by design. He's not alone in his thinking, but he's finding it hard to locate the real-life examples he needs to make his case. In his short lifetime, he's seen some of the largest banks in the world get caught rigging the LIBOR, which is an average interest rate that is used as the main benchmark for global lending rates. Fédération Internationale de Football Association (FIFA) executives were indicted for taking more than $150 million in bribes in exchange for marketing rights. Volkswagen was found guilty of putting software in 11 million cars that manipulated emissions results to make it appear as if the vehicles were passing emissions tests when they were actually failing. Several pharmaceutical manufacturers were found guilty of raising the price of lifesaving drugs by as much as 1,500 percent. Healthcare-testing provider Theranos was found guilty of faking the results of its highly touted blood test to defraud investors. Wells Fargo Bank employees opened 2 million unauthorized accounts to reach sales targets. Still, Sampath believes that it is possible for people in business to have integrity and that it is his mission to help people discover and develop ethical behavior.

Bill and Daniel are new parents, and they've decided to purchase their first home, to give their young family a place to grow. Their credit scores are high, and they both have steady, high-paying jobs. But something keeps happening when they apply for a loan. They're either asked to pay a higher interest rate because of their "risk factors," or declined altogether, with no explanation. "Don't worry," says the mortgage banker they are meeting with today. "Our underwriting is all done by computer. Our algorithms are written to be sure that we make the best decision possible, and there is no risk of human bias coming into play." And yet, they are turned down again.

Luisa had ridden her bike to the grocery store and was on her way home. She had several heavy bags, so it was easier for her to simply walk alongside the bike, now heavy with produce and canned goods, rather than try to balance while riding with her load. She decided to take a shortcut and cross the street on the corner, rather than walking another block to use the pedestrian crosswalk. She saw an opening in the traffic and started across. She had made it across two lanes when the car came along. The human driver wasn't paying attention, and the self-driving vehicle didn't recognize Luisa as a pedestrian because she wasn't where she was supposed to be. She died of her injuries a few hours later. The rideshare company that was testing the technology maintained that Luisa was at fault because she was jaywalking.

Jo is 12 years old. In his country, future careers are determined by one's performance on standardized tests that are administered from childhood to teenage years. Jo wants to be an astronaut, but his aptitude test says he would make a better auto engineer. He is taking courses that are meant to prepare him for his future career and he's doing well. But if he continues on this path, he will attend a technical school instead of college, and will never have the required background needed to enter his country's space program. No one has told Jo that his dream is impossible, but an algorithm has already determined that this is the case.

Alvaro is a young man working in the U.S. Army. He's demonstrated a talent for technology, so he's been trained for a job as an unmanned aircraft systems operator. From his computer station, Alvaro flies unmanned drones for the army, conducting surveillance flights and targeted attacks, as instructed by his senior officers. Alvaro has been trained to study the information on the screen and check for civilians before executing his orders. But in training runs, these images remind him of the characters in his favorite video game, a violent competition that encourages players to hit as many targets as possible in a limited amount of time. In that game, civilians are worth more points than soldiers, and Alvaro is very good at this game. Sometimes, to his horror, he finds himself feeling the same way when he is operating the drone that he feels when he is immersed in the game. He just completed this first mission and neutralized several "targets," achieving his mission and pleasing his commander. Those targets were human beings, fighting against his country on the other side of the world. But it didn't seem real. It felt like just another game on his computer. He wonders if he should tell anyone, but he keeps his concerns to himself.

John is a baker. For 25 years, he's owned and operated his little shop in Poplar Bluff, Missouri. Everyone in town knows when John is baking bread because the wonderful, sweet aroma wafts through every street and sneaks into every window and door. John inherited his shop from his dad, who inherited the same shop from his dad. So John is the third-generation baker in his family. And he'll be the last. John just agreed to sell his business to a large baked-goods manufacturer. The company isn't interested in John and his small production of finely crafted breads, cakes, and cookies. It just wants to eliminate the competition, so it's buying up every bakery within 50 miles of Poplar Bluff. For the folks living in and around the town, this means more jobs, working in the large facility. It's a good living, but it isn't baking, not the way John knows it. The company has offered him a job as a delivery driver, where he'll be visiting the same people who used to come into the shop. John needs the money, so he's considering the job. But life will never be the same for him. And he feels that he has no real choice. Jobs are hard to come by and he has a family to feed.

Aiko used to love coming into the office. She enjoyed working in the open office concept, sharing ideas with the team, telling weekend stories around the coffee maker, and taking a break by walking the beautiful grounds with her friend Michael. Like many people around the world, Aiko was sent home to work during the COVID-19 pandemic. She was issued a laptop and some hurried training, and started working from home every day. Even when things started getting better, Aiko's office was never reopened. Instead, the temporary solution has become the "new normal" for many people, including Aiko. She still enjoys her work and stays in touch with her co-workers online. Aiko's become proficient in her collaboration tools and can videochat or screen share with the best. What Aiko doesn't know is that her employer installed tracking software on her PC. It records every site she visits, every keyboard strike, when she logs on, and when she logs off. If it wants to, her company can study everything she does when she is on their device. It's just one of the "benefits" that came with the technology upgrade it installed to enable its remote workforce.

As long as he can remember, Eli wanted to be a teacher. He got his teaching degree in college but found it hard to land a job. Even though the pay is lousy and the challenges of teaching in the U.S. public-school system are great, there are more would-be teachers than jobs. So Eli brought his talent and passion to corporate training instead. It took him a while to translate his formal training into techniques he could use with adult learners, but soon Eli was one of the top-rated trainers in his field. One of his strongest points is his ability to connect with individual learners in the classroom. His strong presentation style and engaging personality make it easy for him to hold the attention of his audience. But things are changing for Eli and his company. In response to the COVID-19 crisis, Eli was asked to convert all of his classes to online learning. He did his best to think through the delivery of engaging hands-on activities in a virtual environment, and even learned how to make his own videos to "flip" his classroom. Eli's company is getting ready to experiment with several technology-based solutions that will allow it to deliver training online at scale—without a human instructor. They are excited about the vendor's promise to adapt the learning journey to each individual. Eli doesn't know it yet, but he might be out of a job in a year.

Ethics Is Doing the Right Thing

Philosopher, naturalist, and conservationist Aldo Leopold lived between the last days of the American West and the modern era. When he wrote that "ethics is doing the right thing, even when no one else is watching," he was referring to preserving the land and the creatures under our protection who depend on that land, even though no other human being would hold us accountable. His simple definition has become more well known than he is. Nowhere is his definition more fitting than in the world of AI—because no one really is watching. Because they can't.

As humans developed incrementally enhanced technology for studying ourselves, we became aware that something mysterious goes on inside our skulls. The realization that the brain is key to understanding human behavior led to practices that might seem horrifying today, including standard "medical" practices like drilling holes into the skull to treat depression and "reading" the bumps on the head to understand the inner workings of the mind. Today, we are fortunate to live in a world with modern medical devices, vaccines, and cures for many diseases that used to bring almost certain death, and the opportunity to live a long and healthy life. But sometimes I wonder how future generations will assess our current level of care.

Today, there's hypnosis, psychotherapy, and our modern favorite—pharmaceuticals. Each of these treatments is readily available, for anything from weight loss to bipolar disease and schizophrenia. Seen against the backdrop of history, all these efforts to understand and control our minds suggest to me a single fact: We still don't really know what we're doing. We're always just making our best guess about how our brains work. Seen against the totality of what we still need to know, we're barely past where our early ancestors were, wandering in the dark waiting for someone to invent fire.

Geoffrey Hinton, a cognitive psychologist, computer scientist, and one of the great minds behind Google AI, puts it like this: "I have always been convinced that the only way to get artificial intelligence to work is to do the computation in a way similar to the human brain. That is the goal I have been pursuing. We are making progress, though we still have lots to learn about how the brain actually works" (Rosso 2018).

The Origin of Black Box Thinking

In science and engineering, the term *black box* refers to any complex device for which we know the inputs and outputs, but not the inner workings. For example, to many of us, our DVR is a black box. We push the buttons on the remote, select the program we wish to record, and we watch it later. We neither know nor care how it works.

To behaviorists, the mind is a "black box" because we can't know what goes on inside the learner's head. (Or at least we couldn't in 1913, before the birth of neuroscience.) Black box thinking takes a very pragmatic approach to human behavior. All we can do is focus on the stimuli (experiences) that lead to observed behaviors. If we want to encourage certain behaviors, we must deliver stimuli that have been proven to deliver that behavior. Conversely, if we want to change behavior, we must change the stimuli (Watson 2011).

Many forms of artificial intelligence can be called a "black box" because the decision-making process is opaque. It is often impossible to understand exactly how an algorithm makes decisions once it is unleashed on the data that trains it. One reason for this phenomenon is that AI are typically built by companies that need to make a profit. If they reveal the "secret sauce," they'd be out of business, because everyone would be able to replicate their product. I believe that another reason for this difficulty is the nature of the work itself. We have modeled our AI creations after ourselves. And we are the most unknowable thing we know.

B.F. Skinner (1969), one of the "fathers" of behaviorism, put it like this: "The real question is not whether machines think but whether men do. The mystery which surrounds a thinking machine already surrounds a thinking man."

Was he right? Should we focus on inputs and outputs because understanding the black box of AI is beyond our capabilities?

Black box thinking is seductive. It helps us avoid sticky questions that get in the way of achieving practical goals.

It's an elegant means of surrender, if you think about it.

I had a chemistry teacher in high school who required us to show all the steps of our work to answer a problem like "What happens when you combine oxygen with hydrogen?" He once wrote in exasperation on my paper, "Margie, all your answers are correct, but you have arrived at them in completely incorrect ways."

Imagine a machine that thinks like a human, but processes information on a much more efficient scale, by applying algorithms intended to remove any trace of emotion from the process. What "correct" answers might they find that would be correct for all the wrong reasons?

The problem with this approach is that it is an abdication of our responsibility to control the consequences of our choices. And when it comes to AI, the consequences can be dire indeed. I may not need to know how my car works to drive to work tomorrow morning, but I'd sure like to understand how a self-driving car works before I step into one.

Beware the Cobra Effect—Unintended Consequences Are Still Consequences

The cobra effect refers to a well-known tale of how well-meaning people can create horrible consequences by not thinking things through before they act. The real-life story goes like this. While under British rule, India had a problem; the prevalence of cobras on the streets was frightening the English visitors who came to India. To make it a more pleasant environment for visiting Englishmen, the government put a bounty on cobras. For each cobra that was brought in, the government would pay a nice sum. This went on for several months, until some official began to get suspicious. It seemed that no matter how many cobra bounties were paid, there were always at least as many brought in the next week and the week after that. One would think that eventually the population would start to decline. They discovered that something interesting was happening. The locals had started growing cobras to turn in for the bounty. Unwittingly, the government had stimulated an increased production of the very snake they were trying to eliminate. It's such a classic case that it is often taught in economics and ethics classes today.

I was tempted to write that any AI will do exactly what you train it to do, but that's not exactly true. An AI will do exactly what it teaches itself to do by watching what we show it, and therein lies the danger. It learns from us; it replicates our biases and assumptions because humans perform its initial programming (at least for now). When you are using artificial intelligence to develop human talent, there is a serious risk of unintended consequences. The humorous side of this issue is well represented by the popular TED Talk by Janelle Shane. She describes how her program learned to "walk" by breaking itself down into blocks, stacking those blocks on top of one another, and then crashing forward, repeating the process until it reached its goal. When you think about it, this is a perfectly logical solution to the problem. The machine found a perfectly logical and highly efficient means of movement. But it would be a horrible solution for a human being.

John Sumser is the principal analyst at HR Examiner. In a recent article on the ethics of using AI in human resources, he pointed out: "Data is the result of measuring what happens in the world. Our culture is biased. People are biased. Often, they don't even realize it. The data simply reflects this. And trying to bury the signal is the most likely way to amplify it" (Sumser 2020).

When we treat artificial intelligence as an unknowable box that does our bidding, we are blind to the potential consequences of those actions. Here are just a few recent examples of decisions made by AIs that had negative, unintended consequences.

Building AI to Mimic Human Bias

It seemed to make perfect sense. Write an algorithm that can sort through mountains of data to identify which convicts are most likely to become repeat offenders, and which ones have the greatest potential to reform themselves and become valuable contributors to society. The intent was to provide judges with a more reliable way to give deserving people a chance to turn their lives around. Correctional Offender Management Profiling for Alternative Sanctions (COMPAS) is widely used by judges in the U.S. to help them sentence convicted criminals. The tool is designed to conduct a risk assessment of each subject so that the judge can assign a higher sentence to those criminals who represent a higher risk. Although the tool is still in use in 2020, many have questioned its value. At least one study showed that the tool places a higher risk score on black offenders than white offenders, by an almost two to one ratio. Another study demonstrated that the results are statistically no more accurate than crowdsourcing the solution. A group of volunteers online comes up with the same approximate success rate as the AI, about 65 percent.

Raising a Racist on Twitter

In 2016, Microsoft built a chatbot designed to mimic the online conversation of a teenager. The idea was to use live, unfiltered data from Twitter to train "Tay." Microsoft announced the experiment and invited users to engage Tay on the social messaging platform. The plan was to quickly train the AI to improve its conversational skills. And Tay learned a lot from contact with humans. Within a few hours, Tay had learned how to make racial and misogynist slurs with the best of them, even professing admiration for Hitler. When asked "Do you support genocide?" Tay replied, "I do indeed." Microsoft wisely pulled the plug just 20 hours after launching the experiment, but it remains a cautionary tale. When we build an AI to mimic us, we get our flaws as well as our strengths.

Using AI to Evaluate Job Applicants

In a well-publicized case, technology giant Amazon admitted that it had been using an algorithm to sort through resumes to narrow down the pool to a manageable number of candidates for interviews. While the intent was to eliminate unintentional bias against women, the program had the opposite effect. The program was trained on performance data based on 10 years of hiring at Amazon, when the humans made the decisions. The program was taught to identify the résumés of candidates who went on to successful careers at the company, then look for similar patterns in the résumés of new candidates. These résumés were rated from one to five stars, to indicate the likelihood that the candidate would be successful at Amazon. Within a year, it was apparent that the program was favoring men. To its credit, Amazon canceled the program. But what went wrong? The AI was programmed to analyze candidates who had been hired by Amazon to discover the traits that the company valued. That analysis was actually uncovering a long-standing pattern of unconscious bias toward male applicants and identified words and phrases in resumes that tended to be used much more frequently by male applicants. The result was that the program intended to eliminate human bias ended up replicating it.

AI: The Ultimate Plagiarist

David Cope is a musician and an AI expert who has developed Experiments in Musical Intelligence (EMMY) to create new works of music that mimic the style of famous composers. His "new" Vivaldi, for example, worked so well that it was able to fool experts into thinking that the world had discovered a new piece by the human composer. While he has always been very transparent that his work is created as an exercise to advance the science of artificial intelligence, it isn't much of a leap to find a less-scrupulous person using his approach to swindle unsuspecting buyers.

Although it might seem surprising that a computer can mimic the style of an artist, there is a logic behind this approach. Music and art are both highly mathematical in the design and execution of work. Each human artist has a complex, distinguishable pattern. To the human eye or ear, we can learn to recognize the work of an individual artist by their style. When reduced to a pattern by machine learning, style is nothing more than a data set, capturing the patterns that the artist uses to make decisions during the creative process. This same approach has allowed PaintBot to produce a passable Rembrandt or Van Gogh after studying the masters' works for just a few hours.

Why let the arts have all the fun? A college student recently admitted that he used AI to write all his papers using a program originally designed to generate "fake news." Because the program uses actual references and generates text that is based on, but doesn't copy, the work of others, it is almost impossible to detect. In a funny and scathing explanation of how he accomplished this feat, the student pointed out that it was easy to do this because the standards in his graduate business courses are so low. Using AI, he said, is not plagiarism, and he will probably use it again: "The final essay is pretty poor; it's just not poor enough for the professor to fail you."

Editing the Human Genome

Because of its power to sift through data many times faster than human beings, AI is playing a key role in scientific research. One of the most significant contributions of AI was its use to map the human genome, once thought to be an almost impossible task because of our genetic code's complexity. Now that we have the map, geneticists have taken AI to its logical conclusion—editing genes. Gene therapy is finding ways to treat disease by turning off the gene that causes a specific illness or finding the exact regimen that is most likely to work to treat an individual patient for cancer. However, these techniques can be used to make other changes. A scientist in China recently announced the stunning and terrifying achievement of producing two apparently healthy twin girls by manipulating several of their genes before they were born. The original intent was to make them resistant to HIV, but genes are often interconnected. Scientists are still studying how modifying this one trait may have caused other changes in the health or physical makeup of these little girls.

The Ultimate Killing Machine Has No Feelings

It didn't take long for military organizations to recognize the potential for AI to become the ultimate weapon. The U.S. Army is just one of the organizations actively using AI to enhance the capabilities of human troops and, in some cases, replace them in battle. The drones use AI to identify possible targets, and a human operator confirms the data before issuing a "kill shot," which is exactly what it sounds like. The stated intent is to allow more targeted attacks, greatly reducing civilian casualties. However, civilian casualties do occur, and it is unclear whether it is the targeting software or the human operator who is making the mistakes that lead to these unintended deaths. Most likely it is a combination of both. Although a drone on a wild killing spree is the stuff of science fiction for now, the underlying technology for this scenario already exists. In a recent article about the militarization of AI, the *New York Times* recently asked, "Is Ethical Even Possible?"

Make AI Transparent

There's an old saying in the computing industry, "Garbage in, garbage out." The promise of artificial intelligence depends on the quality of the machine learning techniques used to develop it, and these can only be as reliable as the data used for training. Start with tainted data, and you get a tainted result. The data quality problem has been with us since computing began. With the potential for AI to comb through massive amounts of data and make recommendations that affect thousands or millions of lives, the unintended consequences can become dire really quickly. And although we can study the effects of these decisions after the fact, it can be difficult to perform a quality check on the AI on a per-decision basis, because once machine learning is completed, we don't really know how the decision is being made. In his book *Rebooting AI*, cognitive scientist Gary Marcus summarizes our problem:

"There are known knowns and known unknowns, but what we should be worried about most is the unknown unknowns."

Marcus is one of a growing number of "transparent AI" proponents. He calls for taking AI out of the box, making the algorithms publicly available so that they can be widely studied and tested for any possible unintended consequences.

We Need to Make the Rules—But How, and Which Ones?

Scientist and science fiction writer Isaac Asimov imagined a world where intelligent robots took care of and protected the human race. Built into their programming was a set of rules that prevented the robots from doing anything that might harm the humans. His work has influenced science and fiction alike. Many real-life organizations have attempted to build on his idea of hardwiring ethical behavior into robots (a feat we've never quite achieved with human beings). Microsoft's CEO, Satya Nadella, offered this version of these rules:

1. "A.I. must be designed to assist humanity," meaning human autonomy needs to be respected.
2. "A.I. must be transparent," meaning that humans should know and be able to understand how they work.
3. "A.I. must maximize efficiencies without destroying the dignity of people."
4. "A.I. must be designed for intelligent privacy," meaning that it earns trust through guarding their information.
5. "A.I. must have algorithmic accountability so that humans can undo unintended harm."
6. "A.I. must guard against bias" so that they do not discriminate against people.

Notice that the rules tell us what robots and AIs must do, but not how. I also wonder how one teaches an AI to understand "the dignity of people." But hey, it's a start.

This approach is in stark contrast to another set of proposed rules by robotics pioneer Mark Tilden:

1. A robot must protect its existence at all costs.
2. A robot must obtain and maintain access to its own power source.
3. A robot must continually search for better power sources.

In his worldview, it's a survival of the fittest scenario. If a robot or an AI is threatened by humans or finds a superior power source that might harm humans, too bad. The robot must preserve its own existence first.

The truth is, we haven't begun to figure out the ethical complexities of unleashing AI on humanity. This might have been fine if we were still decades away from living with robots, giving us time to put our best minds on the problem and come up with a plan. The trouble is, they're already here, and we often have no idea what they're doing.

So what can we do? As L&D and talent development professionals, we will be on the leading edge of deploying AI in the workplace. We have a responsibility to come up with a plan now for the ethical deployment of these powerful tools. So here are some ideas.

Insist on Algorithmic Transparency

Although the AI profession has come to expect and accept the black box, that is starting to change. Some thought leaders talk about the difference between "opaque" AI and "transparent" AI. The difference is that with transparency, we can understand how the machine has been trained to make decisions, because we have access to the underlying algorithms and the data set(s) used for machine learning. This gives us the opportunity to challenge the underlying assumptions that lead to those decisions.

Oxford professor Sandra Waxter has called for transparency to be supported by regulatory standards and laws.

Transparency doesn't have to apply only to new AI development. In 2016, researchers demonstrated how facial recognition software could be reverse-engineered to reveal the underlying model and even which parts of the model were used in the evaluation of a particular face.

Transparency may even be provided by the AI itself. The Defense Advanced Research Projects Agency, or DARPA, is working on AI systems that can audit themselves and answer queries about how they arrive at decisions. The thinking here is that when it comes to AI, it may "take one to know one."

Building algorithmic, transparent AI requires a change in the way IT professionals approach their work—from initial concept, to machine learning, to implementation. It won't be easy to change the way an entire profession does its work, so we need to be the ones to lead the way. After all, if your company is implementing AI to recruit talent, train employees, evaluate performance, or anything else related to talent development, you are the customer. Insist on a thorough explanation of how the AI will make decisions. (The answer, or lack of one, might surprise you.)

Be Skeptical

Humans aren't the strongest species, nor the fastest. We don't have superior eyesight or super-smelling capabilities. What we do have may not be unique to us, but we certainly have plenty of it—we are hardwired for discovery. The more we question our world, the more we learn about it. Philosopher René Descartes's proposition "I think; therefore, I am" would be better translated as "I doubt; therefore, I think; therefore, I am." The more questions we ask about ourselves, the more answers we'll eventually find. Along the way, we'll find more and more ways to help our black box work more efficiently.

Our first and best defense is probably to be ready to ask the hard questions. We need to be skeptical about any shiny new AI program, even if it's already in use in many other companies. It's possible that you will be the only one asking the hard questions, so you need to be up to the task. You'll find a simple four-step process in the following pages.

You should always ask your AI team about their development and testing process. If you're not satisfied with the answer, this template may be a good place to start.

1. Define exactly what the AI will do.

This might sound obvious, but many buyers of AI solutions focus only on the desired final result, such as "Find the best candidate for the job," or "Handle routine customer complaints." True definition involves describing what decisions the AI will make to identify next steps, what criteria will be used to make those decisions, and where the underlying data will come from. Your development team should be able to walk through examples and demonstrate how the program will address several test cases as part of the definition process.

2. Perform tests to identify any unintended bias in the results.

It has been said that the only way to evaluate the objectivity of a machine might be another machine, but that circular reasoning is just another way of describing AI as an unfathomable black box. If you are considering buying something that the sales team cannot explain in a way that makes sense to you, run! The risk of unintended consequences is just too great.

3. Ask them to perform a "next best decision" test.

AIs are programmed to make the best decision possible every time. Human beings seldom have that luxury. Comparing the "best" decision with the "next best" is one way to identify possible flaws in the underlying logic, or biases that have been accidentally built into the machines by fallible human designers.

4. Run a test on historical data.

Because most AIs are trained on historical data, it is possible to run a test, giving some of that existing data back to the machine as though it is a new instance. The purpose of the test isn't to see if the machine returns the same result; it's to evaluate what result it returns, and whether that result remains true to the original intent of the program.

Sponsor Regulation

Much like AI, rules and regulations can have their own unintended consequences. However, they still provide a necessary foundation. While we can't regulate ethical behavior, we can restrict or discourage unethical behavior through these government regulations and business policies. The European Union General Data Protection Regulation (GDPR) is an example of an attempt to regulate the AI industry, as well as other industries that collect and store private data. The law requires companies to explain exactly how they reach algorithm-based decisions about their customers. For example, if a bank uses algorithms to decide who gets a loan and what interest rate they pay, they must be able to explain what factors go into that decision, how they are weighted, and the process used by the machine to arrive at a decision. They must also document how the humans involved can review the results of the AI to conduct quality control and outline measures to intervene if necessary. Because of the way the law is written, any organization that conducts business with even a single European customer must adhere to the law.

Trust, but Verify

Neuroscience and psychology have taught us that when we expect negative outcomes, we tend to find them. I'm advocating that you become an informed agent for good. By being educated on the potential dangers of AI, you can arm yourself with the tools to identify and implement transparent, ethical uses for this powerful technology in your organization. There is a Russian proverb that former U.S. President Ronald Reagan was fond of quoting when talking about the Soviet Union: "Trust, but verify."

When it comes to artificial intelligence and machine learning, this is the perfect mantra to protect your organization, your employees, and yourself from unintended consequences.

Scientist and AI expert Gary Marcus cautions that "I think that we are entering an era where we are trusting machines more and more, but the machines don't yet deserve that trust—they haven't earned that trust" (Marcus and Davis 2019).

If our creations haven't earned our trust, can we honestly say that we can trust ourselves? One approach may be to find a way to temper the precision of AI with the judgment and compassion of a human being.

If You Can't Beat Them

Computer scientist and mathematician Barbara Grosz sees a different solution. As one of the pioneers in natural language processing, she recommends that AIs be paired with humans to take advantage of the strengths of both and balance the weaknesses of each. When we do this, we get an interesting side effect: the "other AI."

Although computer scientists will continue to pursue true artificial intelligence, another area of exploration is yielding more immediate returns. Augmented cognition is the use of neuroscience to determine a subject's cognitive state in order to enhance it, usually with computers. To me, this is the flip side of artificial intelligence. Instead of trying to make a computer act like the human brain, we try to make our brains a bit more like computers.

DARPA has been interested in this technology for years. Samsung is developing a device to enable people to operate a computer through brain signals. Honeywell has developed a prototype helmet that monitors brain states associated with distraction and information overload. The system produces a visual readout to help commanders understand the cognitive patterns of individual soldiers.

I use a headset to monitor my own brainwaves and maybe eventually control them. With such devices, we might be able to identify the state that psychologist Mihaly Csikszentmihalyi called "flow." This state is often described as a feeling of hyper-learning and well-being (Moor 2020).

In other words, by marrying our brains to computers, we will become the singularity. At this point, it will be pointless to distinguish between silicon-based intelligence and carbon-based intelligence.

It has been said that we are living in the era of the Internet of Everything, meaning that everything will become smarter through connection to the Internet. I'm not sure that the coiners of this term realized they were not just talking about toasters and automobiles.

They were talking about themselves.

Chapter Summary

In this chapter, we discussed the ethical questions of using AI, including:

- black box thinking and unintended consequences—the risks associated with not understanding how an algorithm arrives at a decision
- building transparent AI—a recommendation from many in the field to ensure that explanations of algorithms are widely available to allow for evaluation and troubleshooting
- steps that you can take to make ethical decisions in adopting AI applications
- pairing humans with AI to create the "other AI" of augmented intelligence.

You can find more resources to help you exercise your responsibility to make ethical decisions regarding the AI under your control on the Resource Site.

Deciding how to do the right thing is a shared responsibility. With the potential for great harm or great good, AI is dependent on us to chart the safest and most equitable path forward. We'll explore where we go in our final chapter: "Where Do We Go From Here?"

6

Where Do We Go From Here?

At the beginning of each chapter, we've started with stories that illustrate the subject to be covered. In this final chapter, I'd like to focus on *your* story. Imagine where you will be in 10 years. Now imagine how different your daily life will be. What technological advances do you expect? What changes will you make to your lifestyle? How will you be more productive, healthier, or more secure through technology? Take a moment to paint a picture with your brain. Where does AI fit into this picture? You may be using a digital assistant that takes shape as a hologram or a not-quite-human robot. Or you may be enjoying an exciting job as a creative thought leader while an army of bots takes care of your routine chores. How are you delivering training and consuming education? Have you gone back to school, or finally written that novel, assisted by a helpful content bot that did most of the research and suggested a few paragraphs in the first draft? The story you write can be anything you wish, but thinking doesn't make it happen. The choices you make today will write the story of your tomorrow. I invite you to contemplate a future populated by AI colleagues and employees, in which chats with robots have become commonplace, and connections with your learners are deeply personal and highly agile.

As a learning professional, you will need to pay attention to emerging discoveries in both neuroscience and AI to prepare for the near future of your life and work. Neuroscience teaches us that attention begins with a choice to look in a particular direction. As I mentioned earlier, I believe the COVID-19 crisis will accelerate the development of practical AI, as our war with the coronavirus marshals machine learning to find a treatment and a vaccine. Because AI is already woven into our daily lives, there is little time to spare. We can serve as leaders, helping our organizations adjust to the new reality of an AI-enabled workforce, or we can hold back in ignorance and fear, failing ourselves and the people who depend on us for answers. Here are a few choices you can make today to set your organization on the right path:

- Reboot yourself with a robot.
- Hire a digital assistant.
- Recruit a junior content writer.
- Translate your training with AI.
- Curate your content with AI.
- Manage course registration and payment.
- Get ready for the digital employee.
- Beware the uncanny valley.
- Have a chat with a machine.
- Use a chatbot in your education or training program.
- Deliver performance support at the time of need with a chatbot.
- Challenge the learner to reflect with a chatbot.
- Provide 24/7 performance coaching and support with a chatbot.
- Support new employee onboarding with a chatbot.
- Build a sales coach bot.
- Build a new manager bot.
- Make your LMS smarter.
- Netflix your learning.
- Apply AI to analyze big data and gain big insights.
- Buy a "smart LMS" smartly.
- Plan for your next LMS now.
- Ask better questions.
- Use AI in the recruiting process.
- Train your AI carefully.
- Do the right thing.
- Beware the cobra effect.
- Insist on transparency.
- Be skeptical.
- Insist on a process.
- Sponsor regulation.

- Focus on positive outcomes.
- Trust, but verify.

We've Just Landed in a Strange New World

If all this still seems a bit far-fetched, think of it this way. You've landed on a new planet. Many things are similar to the home you left behind, but other things are surprising, wonderful, puzzling, frustrating, and scary. You booked a one-way trip, so there's no point in wishing you could go back in time. In addition to your new surroundings, you discover to your terror that the planet is already inhabited with creatures who are eerily like you, but deeply different in almost every way. Because you have no way of communicating with them, you can't tell if the natives are friendly or deadly; best to steer clear.

But if you want to survive in this "strange new world," you must begin a relationship with it. Through trial and error, you'll learn what you like about this new home. Thanks to your amazing brain, you have no choice but to explore and adapt, however tentatively at first. Each little victory leads to another, bigger win. And each time you figure something out, your brain gives you a rush of dopamine to say, "Keep going. You're on the right track."

Along the way, you might even run into other castaways who have found their way onto the same planet. Banding together, you can learn from one another, share ideas, and answer one another's questions. You increase your likelihood of surviving and even thriving in this seemingly hostile world by leveraging one of the superpowers of the genus *Apes*—social learning.

Because your genetic code compels you to connect with others, you'll start to be curious about the native creatures on the planet. Over time, you'll learn how to share the planet with them, leverage one another's strengths, and compensate for one another's weaknesses. You'll learn so much that your body will change. You'll develop new skills, and adjust to a new force of gravity and a slightly different, but life-sustaining, atmosphere. Your brain will rewire itself to make you a little more like the native inhabitants, and a little bit less like the people you left behind.

You and your fellow travelers will come to realize that the natives aren't intent on killing you, infecting you, or taking your job. They're just what they are, and you are just who you are.

That's the day you'll realize that your initial feelings of confusion and fear have faded away, replaced by new sensations of understanding and confidence.

The strange new world will have started to feel like home.

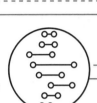

Appendix:
Tools

This section is a curated list of relevant tools, resources, and workshops to learn more about AI and connect with fellow talent development professionals who share your interests. Here you may find additional ATD learning opportunities, chapter events, special interest groups (SIGs), workshops, conferences, and publications, as well as resources pulled from the wider talent development community.

How to Read Any Book and Get More Out of It

There are still times when we really need to read something to gain the information or insight that we seek. In these times, our own brains can conspire against us. The digital world has forced most of us to adapt in ways that make us really poor readers. Changing those habits can be difficult, especially because you may not even be aware that you're doing it.

This checklist should help you (or someone you love) get more out of those books we really need to read, not skim (or just store on our shelves).

How to Read a Book Checklist

Item	Did it!
Tell a friend that you're reading it. This gives you a chance to make a social commitment to another person. You're more likely to finish the book just because you took this first step.	
Review the table of contents before you start. This step helps with a learning concept called priming. It alerts your brain to the topics you'll explore in the book. Just by reading the table of contents, you're stimulating your neural network to begin searching for experiences and information that you already have about each topic.	
Start reading anywhere that interests you. Our digital world works on the science of attention. We pay more attention to things that are of interest to us, or that appeal to our deep programming for survival. Trust your instincts and start wherever your heart (and brain) lead you, to ensure that you begin where your interest is highest.	

How to Read a Book Checklist (cont.)

Item	Did it!
Don't skim! One way to avoid skimming is to read the book aloud to yourself or someone else. This practice has the added approach of slowing you down, because it takes time to pronounce the words. It also gives you the chance to add your own spoken emphasis and tone, helping to make the book your own.	
Take notes by hand (even in the margin if you must). Taking notes has many of the same benefits as reading out loud. As you take notes, you must hold yourself accountable for understanding, questioning, and applying what you're reading. Please resist the urge to simply highlight nearly every sentence of the book, which will only cause distraction, or to type your notes. Many studies demonstrate that taking notes by hand is still the most effective approach.	
Review your notes before moving to the next chapter. Review and revise your notes on a regular basis to help your brain incorporate what you're learning into what you already know and your intentions for action.	
Look up any terms you don't absolutely know. There are many online sources to find the definitions for terms relating to AI. Unfortunately, many of these sources contradict one another. I recommend the Google "Machine Learning Glossary" as a reliable place to begin: developers.google.com/machine-learning/glossary.	

More information available at learningtogo.info/resources.

Idea Starter for Using AI in Talent Development

AI in Talent Development was written to share what I know about the benefits, uses, and risks of artificial intelligence technology in our field. I describe specific actions that can be implemented now to take advantage of innovations in AI-powered talent development and help prepare you and your organization for the evolving AI revolution. As you read this book, capture any ideas that spark the glimmer of a plan, so you can go back and build on these ideas before your brain deletes them from your memory.

My Ideas

Chapter/Section	My idea	Why it matters	How can I begin?
Tips on How to Use This Book			
Chapter 1: Wake Up and Smell the Coffee			
Chapter 2: Reboot Yourself With a Robot			
Chapter 3: Have a Chat With a Machine			
Chapter 4: Make Your Human Capital Management Systems Smarter			
Chapter 5: Do the Right Thing			
Chapter 6: Where Do We Go From Here?			
Conclusion			
Anywhere else			

More information available at learningtogo.info/resources.

Tips for Training Alexa

Alexa is Amazon's digital assistant, via the smart speaker Echo. This information is accurate as of July 27, 2020. Visit learningtogo.info/resources/ for updated information.

Training Alexa

Tasks or Category	Link
Entertainment	tinyurl.com/yyjh5lyg
Communication	tinyurl.com/y3bheck3
Productivity	tinyurl.com/y4ehb8ga
Smart Home	tinyurl.com/yxgfgdd7
Shopping	tinyurl.com/y65bn5bj
News and Information	tinyurl.com/y6yek4u5
Using Multiple Devices	tinyurl.com/y6oxe3na
Things You Can Ask Alexa	tinyurl.com/yxzwv35n

Skills

Skills are like apps that help you do more with Alexa. As with apps, some are available for free and others will cost you a lot of money. Visit the Alexa Skills Store for the latest selection: tinyurl.com/y4zwtcyg.

Blueprints

With Skill Blueprints, you can customize Alexa responses and create personalized skills in minutes: tinyurl.com/yy5t7jkv.

More information available at learningtogo.info/resources.

Tips for Training Siri

Siri is Apple's digital assistant, via any Apple device. Siri comes prepro-grammed with suggestions to streamline your personal and professional life. The program uses emails, calendar appointments, and social media accounts to recognize your routine and tailor suggestions to this routine. These apps are context-specific, so they work differently depending on what you are doing with your device at the time. The more you use the suggestions, the better they will work for you.

You can also create your own workflow to build a customized shortcut.

Resources for Siri Shortcuts

Tasks/Category	Instructions/Link
Siri Shortcuts Gallery (pre-built shortcuts)	Open the Shortcuts app and select Gallery.
Siri Automation (customized workflows)	Open the Shortcuts app and select Automation.
My Shortcuts (previously saved custom workflows)	Open the Shortcuts app and select My Shortcuts.
What can I ask Siri?	https://support.apple.com/siri

This information is accurate as of July 27, 2020. More information and updates are available at learningtogo.info/resources.

Build It or Buy It Decision-Making Tool

In my experience, building moderate to complex solutions in-house is seldom a good idea. They tend to take longer than expected, cost more than originally budgeted, and fail to completely fulfill the purpose they were designed to meet. In addition, building a solution in-house that can be purchased externally distracts your team from doing the work that only they can do.

However, there are some situations where building in-house makes sense. Here's how to assess the "build it or buy" decision.

Instructions:

1. Ask yourself the following questions and rate your response from 0 (low) to 5 (high).
2. Take the total for question set 1 and subtract the total for question set 2.
3. If your result is 0 or less, you may have a case for building in-house.

Question Set 1: How important is it to . . .	Response
Mitigate the risk of errors and rework?	
Adhere to a fixed budget?	
Deliver the solution by a specific date?	
Reduce the costs of maintenance once installed?	
Be on the leading edge of technology?	
Be able to expand the system in the future?	
Total	
Question Set 2: How important is it to . . .	**Response**
Maintain ownership or control of the source code?	
Keep an internal team busy that needs something to do?	
Be compatible with existing equipment and systems?	
Make changes or updates to the system whenever you need them?	
Reuse existing systems or components that were built in-house?	
Spend budgeted funds that you will lose if you don't spend them now?	
Total	

Result	
A. Total score for Question Set 1	
B. Total score for Question Set 2	
C. A minus B	

NOTE: You may add additional questions, but for the scoring to remain accurate, you must always add them in pairs (one to each question set). Visit learningtogo.info/resources for updated information.

How to Choose a Supplier

Use these questions to help select the right supplier to build your AI application. You can modify these questions to suit your needs, and many of them could apply to any type of purchase, so feel free to use this list anytime you need to vet a potential supplier.

Company Background and Support
Please provide a history and overview of your company.
Please provide a list of any customers in our industry and how you have supported them.
Why should we buy from you instead of one of your competitors?
What training will you provide us so that we can manage your solution in-house?
Please describe your customer support model, including expected response times, hours of availability, escalation process, etc.
Please provide any user support materials for our review.

Security
How will you protect our users and our proprietary information?
What level of encryption do you use?
What type of security scans or auditing do you run?
What is your security policy? (Please include a written copy, including passwords, encryption, auditing, alerts, etc.)
What is the procedure for conducting a penetration test (pen test) on your system?
What is your downtime history in the past six months?
Please provide your disaster recovery and business continuity plans.
Where is your data center?
What level of redundancy do your servers and network have?

Chatbot Requirements
Recognize Visitors
Collect User Information (Including custom fields)
Visitor Footprint Tracking
Visitor Contact History
Chat Transcripts and Offline Messages
Post-Chat Satisfaction Survey
Visitor Single Sign-On
Chat Queue and Status
Route Visitors to a Specified Live Operator
Routing to Live Operator (By department, skill, rule-based, load balanced, round robin)

Unlimited Concurrent Chats
Unlimited Canned Messages and URLs
Visual and Sound Alerts
Built-in Spell Checker
Shortcut
Multilevel Canned Responses
Canned Files and Attachments
Emoticon
Typing Indicator
Drag and Drop File Transfer
Screenshot and Image Sending
Automatically End Chats (Timer)
Send Transcript to Email
Built-in Translation Tool
Request Call Back
Voice Chat
Reporting (e.g., Visitors, keywords, visitor location, visitor source, visitor feedback)
Web Analytics (Data from Google Analytics)
Mobile Friendly Chat Window
Integrations/Plug-Ins (Please specify requirements here.)
Pricing Questions
What is the monthly fee for this solution?
What implementation or setup costs can we expect?
Is there a cap or service fee rate for number of visitors or chats?
What will we be charged for support and/or training?
How is your pricing tiered if we want to scale our service up?
What is your cancellation policy?
What guarantees will you provide?
Can we conduct a limited pilot?
Additional Questions (Add your own questions here.)

Additional information at learningtogo.info/resources.

How to Manage a Supplier

Once you've made the decision to seek an outside supplier to provide a learning technology solution, you must be prepared to manage that relationship and forge a strong partnership. As someone who has been on both sides of the equation, here are a few tips for a successful future with your suppliers.

Best Practices

Get to know your supplier's business. Be sure you understand what drives their success.
Get to know your supplier on a personal level. Taking the time to discover what's important to your contacts can make you one of their "favorite clients" in times of crisis.
Set clear expectations in writing as soon as possible. This step prevents misunderstandings later.
Tell your supplier how you will evaluate their performance—in writing.
Conduct regular performance reviews and tell suppliers how well they are doing when compared with other suppliers in similar roles or categories.
Ask your supplier what's working and what isn't every time you meet with them. (And expect them to ask you the same questions.)
Invite your supplier to any meetings that might affect the way they do their work.
Be ready to provide a great review or recommendation when your supplier has earned it.
Make the invoicing process as smooth as possible.
Recognize your suppliers as the experts they are in their fields.
Pay your suppliers on time. Every time. No exceptions.

Additional information at learningtogo.info/resources.

Chatbot Planner

At LearningToGo, we ask three simple questions to start the planning process:

- What problem are you trying to solve?
- Do you know the cause of the problem?
- How could a chatbot help you solve this problem?

Here are a few examples from our customers' responses.

Example 1: Training Completion	
What problem are you trying to solve?	Learners aren't completing our online courses.
Do you know the cause of this problem?	No
How could a chatbot help you solve this problem?	It could collect feedback on the course at the moment when people are leaving it.
Example 2: Learner Engagement	
What problem are you trying to solve?	Learners tell us our courses are boring.
Do you know the cause of this problem?	No
How could a chatbot help you solve this problem?	We could ask learners to rate activities and other content to find out what is most interesting to them.
Example 3: Customer Education	
What problem are you trying to solve?	The company is getting sued because employees aren't reviewing our service offerings and terms accurately and completely at the time of purchase.
Do you know the cause of this problem?	Yes. We have surveyed the sales team and they are reluctant to "slow down" the sales process by delivering this information.
How could a chatbot help you solve this problem?	It could deliver a short review of the terms and gain confirmation that the customer understands and accepts them. This would take the task out of the sales team's hands and make it a consistent part of the ordering process.

Example 4: Develop Sales Skills	
What problem are you trying to solve?	Salespeople are not proficient or confident in handling objections.
Do you know the cause of this problem?	Yes. We have surveyed the sales team and they are reluctant to role play in front of peers or leaders. Thus, they never get any practice handling customer objections until they are in the field.
How could a chatbot help you solve this problem?	It could deliver multiple scenario-based conversations in which the salesperson had to address a common objection to the product or service. The chatbot would respond differently every time, depending on the input provided by the learner. The learner can access the practice bots as many times as needed to gain confidence and learn which approaches are most effective.

Additional information at learningtogo.info/resources

Do You Really Need an LMS?

The right learning management system (LMS) can streamline processes, automate reporting, and provide truly customized learning. But do you really need one? Here are a few questions to ask before your next LMS shopping trip. The more times you check the "yes" column, the more you will benefit from a modern LMS.

Question	Yes	No
Do you have more than 100 employees or learners?		
Do you organize or keep track of your training content?		
Do you need to track completions for business or compliance reasons?		
Do you need to administer, score, and report on objective exams for certification or other purposes?		
Do you need to support customized learning plans by group or individual?		
Do you have a wide variety of methods of delivering your training?		
Do you need help with registration, payment, or other administrative tasks?		
Do you have a remote workforce?		
Does your management measure your effectiveness in part by how many people attended or completed training?		
Do you have multiple people designing content or publishing training?		
Do you deliver proprietary or confidential information in your training?		
Do you sell your training? (Or charge-back internally?)		
Total Responses		

Additional information at learningtogo.info/resources.

Recommended Reading

These resources are not specifically referenced in the book, but I recommend them as further reading about AI in general, and how you can implement AI to support learning and performance in your organization. If you would like to recommend additional resources, please write me at Margie@learningtogo .info, or post your ideas in the space provided on the companion site.

Ako AI. 2018. "How to Test a Chatbot." Medium, July 22. medium.com/@ go.ako.ai/https-akoai-medium-com-how-to-test-a-chatbot-427c55365871.

Baer, J. 2018. "The 6 Critical Chatbot Statistics for 2018." Convince & Convert. convinceandconvert.com/digital-marketing/6-critical-chatbot-statistics -for-2018.

DataNow. 2017. "DataNow Snapshot: Learning Technology Study 2017." Brandon Hall Group, June. go.brandonhall.com/l/8262/2017-06 -05/73hbxx.

Debecker, A. 2017. "2020 Chatbot Statistics—All the Data You Need." Ubisend, August 23. blog.ubisend.com/optimise-chatbots/chatbot-statistics.

Jami, J. 2018. "What's Big in Chatbots in 2018 and Beyond." BotCore, January 11. botcore.ai/blog/whats-big-chatbots-2018-beyond.

Jenewein, T. 2017. "Machine Learning: 7 Use Cases for Education & Learning." SAP Community, July 26. blogs.sap.com/2017/07/26/machine -learning-7-use-cases-for-education-learning.

Learning Guild, The. 2018. "Artificial Intelligence Across Industries: Where Does L&D Fit?" The Learning Guild, August 16. learningguild.com /insights/226/artificial-intelligence-across-industries-where-does-ld -fit/?utm_campaign=research-ai18&utm_medium=link&utm_ source=lspub.

Marr, B. n.d. "Making Products Smarter With Artificial Intelligence." Bernard Marr & Co. bernardmarr.com/default.asp?contentID=730.

Meacham, M. 2018. "Will a Chatbot Be Your Next Learning Coach? How AI Can Support Talent Development in Your Organization." LearningToGo, January 15. learningtogo.info/2018/01/15/will-a-chatbot-be-your -next-learning-coach-how-ai-can-support-talent-development-in-your -organization.

Penenberg, A. 2010. "Social Networking Affects Brains Like Falling in Love." *Fast Company*, July 1. fastcompany.com/1659062/social-networking-affects -brains-falling-love.

Rosenberg, M. 2013. "At the Moment of Need: The Case for Performance Support." The Learning Guild, June 6. learningguild.com/publications/ index.cfm?id=33&utm_campaign=wp-ps1306&utm_medium=link&utm_ source=lsm-news.

Satow, L. 2017. "Chatbots as Teaching Assistants: Introducing a Model for Learning Facilitation by AI Bots." SAP Community, July 12. blogs.sap .com/2017/07/12/chatbots-as-teaching-assistants-introducing-a-model-for -learning-facilitation-by-ai-bots.

Schaffhauser, D. 2018. "Experts Weigh in on Merits of AI in Education." The Journal, December 20. thejournal.com/articles/2018/12/20/experts -debate-merits-of-ai-in-education.aspx.

University of Toronto. n.d. "The Turing Test." psych.utoronto.ca/users /reingold/courses/ai/turing.html.

Zak, P. 2008. "The Neurobiology of Trust." *Scientific American*, June. scientificamerican.com/article/the-neurobiology-of-trust.

References

Introduction

Deaton, S. 2015. "Social Learning Theory in the Age of Social Media: Implications for Educational Practitioners." *Journal of Educational Technology* 12(1): 1–6.

DeBrule, S. 2020. "Machine Learnings: Understand How AI Will Change Your Work and Life." Newsletter. subscribe.machinelearnings. co/?utm_source=machine_learnings&utm_medium=blog&utm_campaign=publication_homepage&utm_content=navigation_cta.

Google. 2019. "The Machine Learning Glossary." developers.google.com/machine-learning/glossary/.

Mueller, P.A., and D.M. Oppenheimer. 2014. "The Pen Is Mightier Than the Keyboard: Advantages of Longhand Over Laptop Note Taking." *Psychological Science* 25(6): 1159-68.

Niiler, E. 2020. "An Epidemiologist Sent the First Warnings of the Wuhan Virus." *Wired,* January 25. wired.com/story/ai-epidemiologist-wuhan-public-health-warnings/.

Opong, T. 2017. "The Life-Changing Habit of Journaling (Why Einstein, Leonardo da Vinci, and Many More Great Minds Recommend it)." *Medium,* June 22. medium.com/thrive-global/start-journaling-54ea2edb104.

Wolf, M. 2018. "Skim Reading Is the New Normal. The Effect on Society Is Profound." *The Guardian,* August 25. theguardian.com/commentisfree/2018/aug/25/skim-reading-new-normal-maryanne-wolf.

Chapter 1

Anderson, M.R. 2017. "Twenty Years on From Deep Blue vs Kasparov: How a Chess Match Started the Big Data Revolution." *The Conversation,* May 11. theconversation.com/twenty-years-on-from-deep-blue-vs-kasparov-how-a-chess-match-started-the-big-data-revolution-76882.

Baer, J. 2018. "The 6 Critical Chatbot Statistics for 2018." *Convince & Convert.* convinceandconvert.com/digital-marketing/6-critical-chatbot -statistics-for-2018.

Best, J. 2013. "IBM Watson: The Inside Story of How the Jeopardy-Winning Supercomputer Was Born, and What It Wants to Do Next." *TechRepublic,* September 9. techrepublic.com/article/ibm-watson-the-inside-story-of -how-the-jeopardy-winning-supercomputer-was-born-and-what-it-wants -to-do-next.

Brandon Hall Group. 2016. "Learning Technology." Brandon Hall. go.brandonhall.com/l/8262/2016-04-25/5brswr.

Business Wire. 2018. "Worldwide Spending on Cognitive and Artificial Intelligence Systems Forecast to Reach $77.6 Billion in 2022, According to New IDC Spending Guide." *Business Wire,* September 19. businesswire .com/news/home/20180919005045/en/Worldwide-Spending-Cognitive -Artificial-Intelligence-Systems-Forecast.

Chalmers, D.J. 1995. "Facing Up to the Problem of Consciousness." *Journal of Consciousness Studies* 2(3): 200–19.

Chawla, V. 2019. "How China Is Revolutionising Education Using Artificial Intelligence." *Analytics India Magazine,* August 26. analyticsindiamag. com/china-artificial-intelligence-education.

Chowdhury, H. 2020. "Could We Ever Create an AI as Smart as the Human Brain?" *The Telegraph,* January 16. telegraph.co.uk/technology/ 2020/01/15/can-googles-british-sister-company-deepmind-build -computer-smart.

Ciccarelli, M. 2020. "Humans Plus AI Improves Cybersecurity Risk Response." *Human Resource Executive,* January 2. hrexecutive.com/ humans-plus-ai-improves-cybersecurity-risk-response.

Davies, S. 2018. "Artificial Intelligence Is Changing the Translation Industry. But Will It Work?" *Digitalist Magazine,* July 6. digitalistmag.com /digital-economy/2018/07/06/artificial-intelligence-is-changing- translation-industry-but-will-it-work-06178661.

Degreed and Harvard Business Publishing. 2019. *How the Workforce Learns in 2019*. harvardbusiness.org/insight/how-the-workforce-learns-in-2019.

Dillon, JD. 2020. "The Path to AI." *TD*, January. td.org/td-magazine/january-2020-td-magazine.

Encyclopedia Britannica. n.d. "Thomas Bayes." britannica.com/biography/Thomas-Bayes.

Farnam Street Blog. 2013. "The Original Parkinson's Law and the Law of Triviality." Farnam Street Blog. fs.blog/2013/12/parkinsons-law.

Georgia Tech. n.d. "Georgia Tech's Emprize: AI-Powered Learning. Anytime. Anywhere." emprize.gatech.edu.

Goren, E. 2003. "America's Love Affair With Technology: The Transformation of Sexuality and the Self Over the 20th Century." *Psychoanalytic Psychology* 20(3): 487-508.

Gratton, L., D. Rock, J. Voelker, and T. Welsh. 2019. "Redefining the Role of the Leader in the Reskilling Era." *McKinsey Quarterly,* December.

Hassabis, D., D. Kumaran, C. Summerfield, and M. Botvinick. 2017. "Neuroscience-Inspired Artificial Intelligence." *Neuron* 95(2): 245-58.

Ismail, N. 2019. "The History of the Chatbot: Where It Was and Where It's Going." *Information Age,* February 11.

Jackson, N. 2011. "Electro the Moto-Man, One of the World's First Celebrity Robots." *The Atlantic,* February 21. theatlantic.com/technology/archive/2011/02/elektro-the-moto-man-one-of-the-worlds-first-celebrity-robots/71505.

Kamarck, E. 2018. "Malevolent Soft Power, AI, and the Threat to Democracy." Brookings Institution, November 29. brookings.edu/research/malevolent-soft-power-ai-and-the-threat-to-democracy.

Kasinathan, G., and K.S. Yogesh. 2019. Exploring AI in Indian School Education. National Seminar on "Innovative Practices and Research in the Era of Digi Education," March 21–22. itforchange.net/sites/default/files/2019-08/Paper-AI-and-education-Seminar-by-UOH-March-20-2019-with-abstract.pdf.

Koch, M. 2017. "The Turing Test: The History Behind Measuring Artificial Intelligence." *Medium,* May 12. medium.com/@MichaelKoch/the-turing-test-the-history-behind-measuring-artificial-intelligence-284efa636c3b.

Life Sciences Trainers & Educators Network (LTEN). 2019. "Artificial Intelligence: The Future of Work?" LTEN, January 24. lten-industrybrief.caboodleai.net/en/article/22742.

Georgia Tech 2020. "Jill Watson, an AI Pioneer in Education, Turns 4." ic.gatech.edu/news/631545/jill-watson-ai-pioneer-education-turns-4.

Marr, B. 2018. "How Much Data Do We Create Every Day? The Mind-Blowing Stats Everyone Should Read." *Forbes,* May 21. forbes.com/sites/bernardmarr/2018/05/21/how-much-data-do-we-create-every-day-the-mind-blowing-stats-everyone-should-read/#3204496d60ba.

Marsh, A. 2018. "Electro the Moto-Man Had the Biggest Brain at the 1939 World's Fair." IEEE Spectrum, September 28. spectrum.ieee.org/tech-history/dawn-of-electronics/elektro-the-motoman-had-the-biggest-brain-at-the-1939-worlds-fair.

Martin, N. 2019. "Did a Robot Write This? How AI Is Impacting Journalism." *Forbes,* February 8. forbes.com/sites/nicolemartin1/2019/02/08/did-a-robot-write-this-how-ai-is-impacting-journalism/#6f9139857795.

McCarthy, J., M.L. Minsky, N. Rochester, and C.E. Shannon. 1955. "A Proposal for the Dartmouth Summer Research Project on Artificial Intelligence." formal.stanford.edu/jmc/history/dartmouth/dartmouth.html.

McCulloch, W.S., and W. Pitts. 1943. "A Logical Calculus of the Ideas Immanent in Nervous Activity." *The Bulletin of Mathematical Biophysics* 5, 115–33. link.springer.com/article/10.1007/BF02478259.

Meacham, M. 2017. "What Does It Mean to Be Intelligent?" LearningToGo. learningtogo.info/2017/06/09/what-does-it-mean-to-be-intelligent-2.

Miner, N. 2018. *Future-Proofing Your Organization by Teaching Thinking Skills: A Survival Guide for 21st Century Business.*

MIT Technology Review. 2017. "Artificial Intelligence Can Translate Languages Without a Dictionary." *MIT Technology Review.* technologyreview.com/f/609595/artificial-intelligence-can-translate-languages-without-a-dictionary.

Nadkarni, P.M., L. Ohno-Machado, and W.W. Chapman. 2011. "Natural Language Processing: An Introduction." *Journal of the American Medical Informatics Association* 18(5): 544–51. doi.org/10.1136/amiajnl-2011-000464.

Naveen, J. 2019. "How Far Are We From Achieving Artificial General Intelligence?" *Forbes,* June 10.

Nessier, U. 1979. "The Concept of Intelligence." *Intelligence* 3(3): 217–27.

PBS. N.d. "Tesla: Life and Legacy." pbs.org/tesla/ll/ll_robots.html.

Pfeiffer, U., B. Timmermans, K. Vogeley, C. Frith, and L. Schilbach. 2013. "Towards a Neuroscience of Social Interaction." *Frontiers in Human Neuroscience*, February 1. frontiersin.org/articles/10.3389/fnhum.2013.00022/full.

Popova, M. 2015. "How Ada Lovelace and Charles Babbage Invented the World's First Computer: An Illustrated Adventure in Footnotes and Friendship." *Brainpickings*. brainpickings.org/2015/06/15/the-thrilling-adventures-of-lovelace-and-babbage-sydney-padua.

Russell, J. 2017. "Google's AlphaGo AI Wins Three-Match Series Against World's Best Go Player." *TechCrunch,* May 25. techcrunch.com/2017/05/24/alphago-beats-planets-best-human-go-player-ke-jie.

Ryan, K.J. 2018. "This Robot Detects Lung Cancer Better Than Any Human Doctor—And That's Just for Starters." *Inc.,* July/August. inc.com/magazine/201808/kevin-j-ryan/monarch-platform-auris-health.html.

Sagan, C. 2002. *Cosmos.* New York: Random House.

Simon, M. 2018. "The WIRED Guide to Robots." *Wired,* May 15. wired.com/story/wired-guide-to-robots.

Sivasubramanian, S. 2020. "How AI and Machine Learning Are Helping to Fight COVID-19." The World Economic Forum COVID Action Platform, May 28. weforum.org/agenda/2020/05/how-ai-and-machine-learning-are-helping-to-fight-covid-19.

Starner, T. 2020. "Fortune 500 Study: Personalization, AI Deficit in Job Candidate Experience." *Human Resource Executive,* January 17.

Sternberg, R.J., and J.C. Kaufman. 2002. *Intelligence: Encyclopedia of the Human Brain.*

Straders, A. 2019. "What Is Artificial Intelligence? Examples and News in 2019." *TheStreet,* January 3. thestreet.com/technology/what-is-artificial-intelligence-14822076.

Tracxn. 2019. "Artificial Intelligence Startups in India." tracxn.com/explore/Artificial-Intelligence-Startups-in-India.

Turing, A.M. 1950. "Computing Machinery and Intelligence." *Mind* 59(236): 433–60.

University of Reading. 2014. "Turing Test Success Marks Milestone in Computing History." reading.ac.uk/news-archive/press-releases/pr583836.html.

Van Dinteren, R., K. Nijsman, and M. Meacham. 2018. "From Learning to Performance: Global Lessons from the Brain Ladies." Whitepaper. brainladies.com/homepages/whitepaper.

Wired. 2017. "The Robot Will See You Now." *Wired,* April 25. youtu.be/x1Qu1YKZA0Y.

Chapter 2

Anderson, G., J. Thomas, and J. Katzenbach. 2018. *The Critical Few: Energize Your Company's Culture by Choosing What Really Matters.* Oakland, CA: Berrett-Koehler.

Berger, G. 2019. *The Jobs of Tomorrow: LinkedIn's 2020 Emerging Jobs Report.* LinkedIn. blog.linkedin.com/2019/december/10/the-jobs-of-tomorrow-linkedins-2020-emerging-jobs-report.

Bersin, J. 2019. "AI in the Flow of Work. Insights on Corporate Talent, Learning, and HR Technology." Josh Bersin, January 2. joshbersin.com/2018/11/learning-in-the-flow-of-work-arriving-now.

Borden, T., and A. Akhtar. 2020. "The Coronavirus Has Triggered Unprecedented Mass Layoffs and Furloughs. Here Are the Major Companies That Are Downsizing Their Workforces." *Business Insider,* May 28. businessinsider.com/coronavirus-layoffs-furloughs-hospitality-service-travel-unemployment-2020.

Brandon Hall Group. 2017. *Learning Technology Study 2017.* go.brandonhall.com/l/8262/2017-06-05/73hbxx.

Branson, R.K., G.T. Rayner, J.L. Cox, J.P. Furman, F.J. King, and W.H. Hannum. 1975. "Interservice Procedures for Instructional Systems Development, Vols. 1-5." TRADOC Pam 350-30, NAVEDTRA 106A. Ft. Monroe, VA: U.S. Army Training and Doctrine Command.

Caballar, R.D. 2019. "What Is the Uncanny Valley?" IEEE Spectrum, November 6. spectrum.ieee.org/automaton/robotics/humanoids/what-is-the-uncanny-valley.

Cohen, J.N., and P. Mihailidis. 2013. "Exploring Curation as a Core Competency in Digital and Media Literacy Education." *Faculty Works: Digital Humanities & New Media 4.* digitalcommons.molloy.edu/dhnm_fac/4.

Darlington, K. 2020. "How Artificial Intelligence Is Helping Prevent the Spread of the COVID-19 Pandemic." *OpenMind BBVA,* May 22. bbvaopenmind.com/en/technology/artificial-intelligence/how-ai-is-helping-prevent-the-spread-of-the-covid-19-pandemic.

Frey, C.B., and M.A. Osborne. 2013. "The Future of Employment: How Susceptible Are Jobs to Computerisation?" Oxford University Engineering Sciences Department and the Oxford Martin Programme on the Impacts of Future Technology. "Machines and Employment" Workshop, September 17.

Friedman, M. 2015. "There's a Deeply Scientific Reason That Siri's Voice Is Female." *Marie Claire,* October 30. marieclaire.com/culture/news/a16682/why-is-siri-a-female-voice.

Hernández-Orollo, J. 2020. "AI Evaluation: On Broken Yardsticks and Measurement Scales." Association for the Advancement of Artificial Intelligence. eval.how/aaai-2020/REAIS19_p14.pdf.

Kelly, P. 2016. "Transforming Assessment Into Great Learning Experiences." Ed.gov Blog. blog.ed.gov/2016/12/transforming-assessment-into-great-learning-experiences.

Lowrey, A. 2018. "Wages Are Low, and Workers Are Scare. Wait, What?" *The Atlantic,* September 19. theatlantic.com/ideas/archive/2018/09/is-america-facing-a-labor-shortage/570649.

Manjoo, F. 2013. "You Won't Finish This Article," *Slate,* June. slate.com/technology/2013/06/how-people-read-online-why-you-wont-finish-this-article.html.

Marr, B. 2018. "How Much Data Do We Create Every Day? The Mind-Blowing Stats Everyone Should Read," *Forbes,* May 21. forbes.com/sites/bernardmarr/2018/05/21/how-much-data-do-we-create-every-day-the-mind-blowing-stats-everyone-should-read/#42e9139260ba.

McKinsey & Company. n.d. "The Next Normal." McKinsey & Company. mckinsey.com/featured-insights/the-next-normal.

Norcross, J.C., G.P. Koocher, and A. Garofalo. 2006. "Discredited Psychological Treatments and Tests: A Delphi Poll." *Professional Psychology: Research and Practice* 37(5): 515-22. doi:10.1037/0735-7028.37.5.515.

Paul, R., and L. Elder. 1997. Foundation for Critical Thinking. criticalthinking.org.

Rodgers, C. 2002. "Defining Reflection: Another Look at John Dewey and Reflective Thinking." pdfs.semanticscholar. org/8306/5a718ecebe57d7dea8a80f6d2a746c7b7a86.pdf.

Sneader, K., and S. Singhal. 2020. "Beyond Coronavirus: The Path to the Next Normal." McKinsey & Company, March 23. mckinsey.com/ industries/healthcare-systems-and-services/our-insights/beyond-coronavirus-the-path-to-the-next-normal.

Srdanovic, B. 2018. "Educational Chatbots and the Use of Instant Messaging Apps in the Classroom." eLearning Industry, March 24. elearningindustry.com/educational-chatbots-use-instant-messaging-apps-classroom.

Tansey, I. 2017. "Bots vs. Robots: What's the Difference?" Codebots. codebots.com/artificial-intelligence/robots-and-bots-explained.

Villar, C. Creating. 2017. "Conversational Experiences (II)." *Medium,* December 12. medium.com/landbot-io/creating-conversational-experiences-ii-build-and-design-20ac88d7ee72.

Chapter 3

Devaney, E. 2018. "The State of Chatbots Report: How Chatbots Are Reshaping Online Experiences." Drift, January 23. drift.com/blog/ Chatbots-report.

Editorial Team. 2018. "How Netflix Uses Big Data to Drive Success." Inside Big Data, January 20. insidebigdata.com/2018/01/20/netflix-uses-big-data-drive-success.

Herr, N. 2007. "Internet Resources to Accompany the Sourcebook for Teaching Science." csun.edu/science/health/docs/tv%26health.html.

McFadden, C. 2019. "How Exactly Does Netflix Recommend Movies to You?" Interesting Engineering, June 3. interestingengineering.com/how-exactly-does-netflix-recommend-movies-to-you.

Sullivan, D. 2018. "How Google Autocomplete Works in Search." Google Search Blog. blog.google/products/search/how-google-autocomplete-works-search.

Turing, A. 1950. "Computing Machinery and Intelligence." *Mind* 49:433–60. csee.umbc.edu/courses/471/papers/turing.pdf.

Ulanoff. L. 2014. "Amazon Knows What You Want Before You Buy It." *Machine Learning Times,* January 27. predictiveanalyticsworld.com/ machinelearningtimes/amazon-knows-what-you-want-before-you-buy-it.

Chapter 4

ATD Research. 2018. *Is the LMS Dead? Learning Management Technology in Today's Organizations.* Alexandria, VA: ATD Press.

Blattmann, J. 2018. "Netflix: Binging on the Algorithm." *Medium,* August 2. uxplanet.org/netflix-binging-on-the-algorithm-a3a74a6c1f59.

Brandon Hall Group. 2016. *2016 Learning Technology Study.* tinyurl.com/zysxev7.

Dawkins, R. 1976. *The Selfish Gene.* New York: Oxford University Press.

Dawson, T. 2019. "Learning, Emotion, and the Goldilocks Zone." *Medium,* March 10. medium.com/@theo_dawson/learning-emotion-and-the-goldilocks-zone-30295765dd7a.

Dickson, B. 2019. "What Is Deep Learning?" *PCMag,* August 8. pcmag.com/news/what-is-deep-learning.

Expertus. 2007. "Expertus Survey Reveals Executive Frustration With Learning Measurement." Expertus. expertus.com/81-of-lms-users-are-dissatisfied-with-reporting.

Herold, B. 2020. "The Scramble to Move America's Schools Online." *Edweek,* March 27. edweek.org/ew/articles/2020/03/26/the-scramble-to-move-americas-schools-online.html.

Johnson, K. 2019. "How Google Maps Uses Machine Learning to Predict Bus Traffic Delays in Real Time." *Venture Beat,* June 27. venturebeat.com/2019/06/27/how-google-maps-uses-machine-learning-to-predict-bus-traffic-delays-in-real-time.

Kirkpatrick, J.D., and W.K. Kirkpatrick. 2016. *Kirkpatrick's Four Levels of Training Evaluation.* Alexandria, VA: ATD Press.

Kodak Workflow Documentation. 2019. "What Is Rules-Based Automation?" Kodak Workflow Documentation. workflowhelp.kodak.com/pages/viewpage.action?pageId=40208668.

Koidan, K. 2019. "How Netflix Uses Contextually-Aware Algorithms to Personalize Movie Recommendations." Topbots, June 26. topbots.com/netflix-movie-recommender-system-rework.

McIlvaine, A. 2020. "Technology's Role in Recruitment." *Human Resource Executive,* May 19. hrexecutive.com/technologys-role-in-recruitment/?eml=20200529&oly_enc_id=5023D9664490H1Z.

Meacham, M. 2017. "The Near Future of Learning Automation: The Smart LMS." ATD Insights, April 27. td.org/insights/the-near-future-of-learning-automation-the-smart-lms.

Olckers, A. 2020. "AI in War: 'Algorithms Will Fight Each Other in 20 Years.'" *Medium,* March 7. medium.com/swlh/ai-in-war-algorithms-will-fight-each-other-in-20-years-4df66b346826.

Pandey, P. 2020. "Recommendation Systems in the Real World." Topbots, January 29. topbots.com/recommendation-systems-in-the-real-world.

Pappas, C. 2020. "Anytime, Anywhere Learning Essentials: 5 Features That Your Next LMS App Must Include." *eLearning Industry,* January 18. elearningindustry.com/next-lms-app-features-must-include-anytime-anywhere-learning.

Psychology Today. N.d. "Social Learning Theory." *Psychology Today.* psychologytoday.com/us/basics/social-learning-theory.

Selyukh, A. 2018. "Optimized Prime: How AI and Anticipation Power Amazon's 1-Hour Deliveries." *NPR Morning Edition,* November 21. npr.org/2018/11/21/660168325/optimized-prime-how-ai-and-anticipation-power-amazons-1-hour-deliveries.

Seseri, R. 2018. "How AI Is Changing the Game for Recruiting." *Forbes,* January 29. forbes.com/sites/valleyvoices/2018/01/29/how-ai-is-changing-the-game-for-recruiting/#389dc2a21aa2.

Shekhtman, L. 2019. "NASA Takes a Cue From Silicon Valley to Hatch Artificial Intelligence Technologies." NASA, November 25. nasa.gov/feature/goddard/2019/nasa-takes-a-cue-from-silicon-valley-to-hatch-artificial-intelligence-technologies.

Smyth, A. 2019. "How Artificial Intelligence (AI) in Learning Management Systems (LMS) Will Streamline Employee Learning." *HR Technologist,* April 26. hrtechnologist.com/articles/learning-development/how-artificial-intelligence-in-learning-management-systems-will-streamline-employee-learning.

Thomson, A. 2020. "Google Shows AI Can Spot Breast Cancer Better Than Doctors." *Bloomberg,* January 2. bloomberg.com/news/articles/2020-01-02/google-shows-ai-can-spot-breast-cancer-better-than-doctors.

Williamson, J. n.d. "The 4 V's of Big Data." dummies.com/careers/find-a-job/the-4-vs-of-big-data.

Chapter 5

———. n.d. "Behaviorism: A Psychological Perspective." PSU. personal.psu. edu/wxh139/bahavior.htm.

———. 2019. "Gary Marcus on Why AI Needs a Reboot." *Psychology Today,* September 20. psychologytoday.com/us/blog/the-future-brain/201909/ gary-marcus-why-ai-needs-reboot.

Abadicio, M. 2019. "Artificial Intelligence in the U.S. Army—Current Initiatives." *Emerj,* November 22. emerj.com/ai-sector-overviews/ artificial-intelligence-in-the-us-army.

Asimov, I. 2009. "The Three Laws of Robotics." George Law YouTube Channel, March 4. youtube.com/watch?v=AWJJnQybZlk.

Bleicher, A. 2017. "Demystifying the Black Box That Is AI." *Scientific American,* August 9. scientificamerican.com/article/demystifying-the-black-box-that-is-ai.

Bordalo, P., N. Gennaioli, and A. Shleifer. 2017. "Memory, Attention and Choice." Ideas. ideas.repec.org/p/nbr/nberwo/23256.html.

Cherry, K. 2020. "How a Phrenology Head Was Traditionally Used." *Verywell Mind,* March 31. verywellmind.com/example-and-overview-of-a-phrenology-head-4111124.

Comen, E., and T.C. Frohlich. 2019. "The Biggest Corporate Scandals of the Decade." 24/7 Wall St., December 20. 247wallst.com/special-report/2019/12/20/the-biggest-corporate-scandals-of-the-decade/3.

Dastin, J. 2018. "Amazon Scraps Secret AI Recruiting Tool That Showed Bias Against Women." *Reuters,* October 9. reuters.com/article/us-amazon-com-jobs-automation-insight/amazon-scraps-secret-ai-recruiting-tool-that-showed-bias-against-women-idUSKCN1MK08G.

Davies, A., and J.R. Harrigan. 2019. "The Cobra Effect: Lessons in Unintended Consequences." Foundation for Economic Education, September 6. fee.org/articles/the-cobra-effect-lessons-in-unintended-consequences.

DreamWorks Wiki. n.d. "Hiccup/Quotes." DreamWorks. dreamworks. fandom.com/wiki/Hiccup/Quotes.

Dressel, J., and H. Farid. 2018. "The Accuracy, Fairness, and Limits of Predicting Recidivism." *Science Advances,* January 17. advances. sciencemag.org/content/4/1/eaao5580.

Epstein, Z., H.P. Blakeley, J. Hanwen Shen, A. Dubey, B. Felbo, M. Groh, N. Obradovich, M. Cebrian, and I. Rahwan. "Closing the AI Knowledge Gap." Cornell University, March 20. arxiv.org/abs/1803.07233.

Garcia, C. 2015. "Algorithmic Music—David Cope and EMI." Computer History Museum, April 29. computerhistory.org/blog/algorithmic-music-david-cope-and-emi.

Goyal, Y., A. Mohapatra, D. Parikh, and D. Batra. 2016. "Towards Transparent AI Systems: Interpreting Visual Question Answering Models." Cornell University. https://arxiv.org/abs/1608.08974.

Greene, T. 2019. "Researchers Were About to Solve AI's Black Box Problem, Then the Lawyers Got Involved." TNW, December 17. thenextweb.com/artificial-intelligence/2019/12/17/researchers-were-about-to-solve-ais-black-box-problem-then-the-lawyers-got-involved.

Leopold, A. 1949. *A Sand County Almanac: And Sketches Here and There.* New York: Oxford University Press.

Marcus, G., and E. Davis. 2019. *Rebooting AI: Building Artificial Intelligence We Can Trust.* New York: Vintage.

Moore, C. 2020. "What Is Flow in Psychology?" *Positive Psychology.* positivepsychology.com/what-is-flow.

Nadella, S. 2016. "The Partnership of the Future." *Slate,* June 28. slate.com/technology/2016/06/microsoft-ceo-satya-nadella-humans-and-a-i-can-work-together-to-solve-societys-challenges.html.

Pasztor, A. 2007. "Honeywell Tests Brain-Wave System." International Military Forum, November 13. military-quotes.com/forum/honeywell-tests-brain-wave-system-t48014.html.

Randall, I. 2019. "AI Gets Painting Down to a Fine Art as Algorithm Learns to Mimic the Unique Styles and Brushstrokes of Master Artists Including Van Gogh, Vermeer, and Turner." *Daily Mail,* April 26. dailymail.co.uk/sciencetech/article-6963651/AI-learns-mimic-unique-styles-master-artists-including-Van-Gogh-Vermeer-Turner.html.

Regalado, A. 2019. "China's CRISPR Twins Might Have Had Their Brains Inadvertently Enhanced." *MIT Technology Review,* February 21. technologyreview.com/2019/02/21/137309/the-crispr-twins-had-their-brains-altered.

Robitzski, D. 2020. "This Grad Student Used a Neural Network to Write His Papers." *Futurism,* April 21. futurism.com/grad-student-neural-network-write-papers.

Robot Staff. 2010. "The Evolution of a Roboticist—Mark Tilden." Robot, December 7. botmag.com/the-evolution-of-a-roboticist-mark-tilden.

Rojahn, S.Y. 2013. "Samsung Demos a Tablet Controlled by Your Brain." *MIT Technology Review,* April 19. technologyreview.com/2013/04/19/253309/samsung-demos-a-tablet-controlled-by-your-brain.

Rosso, C. 2018. "20 Great Quotes on Artificial Intelligence." *Psychology Today,* May 18. psychologytoday.com/us/blog/the-future-brain/201805/20-great-quotes-artificial-intelligence.

Shane, J. 2019. "The Danger of AI Is Weirder Than You Think." TED2019. ted.com/talks/janelle_shane_the_danger_of_ai_is_weirder_than_you_think?language=en.

Shaw, J. 2019. "Artificial Intelligence and Ethics." *Harvard Magazine,* January–February. harvardmagazine.com/2019/01/artificial-intelligence-limitations.

Skinner, B.F. 1969. *Contingencies of Reinforcement: A Theoretical Analysis.* New York: Appleton-Century-Crofts.

Sumser, J. 2020. "8 Ways to Reflect on Your HR Ethics." *Human Resource Executive,* June 4. hrexecutive.com/sumser-8-ways-to-reflect-on-your-hr-ethics.

Vincent, J. 2016. "Twitter Taught Microsoft's AI Chatbot to Be a Racist Asshole in Less Than a Day." *The Verge,* March 24. theverge.com/2016/3/24/11297050/tay-microsoft-chatbot-racist.

Wachter, S., B. Mittelstadt, and L. Floridi. 2017. "Transparent, Explainable, and Accountable AI for Robotics." *Science Robotics* 2(6). philarchive.org/archive/WACTEA.

Watson, J.B., and W. McDougall. 1929. *Behaviorism.* New York: W.W. Norton.

WhatIs.com. 2019. "Black Box AI." WhatIs.com. whatis.techtarget.com/definition/black-box-AI.

Wigan, M. 2019. "Rethinking IT Professional Ethics." Australian Institute of Computer Ethics Conference. researchgate.net/profile/Marcus_Wigan/publication/341656019_Rethinking_IT_Professional_Ethics/links/5ecdb0cf4585152945146f00/Rethinking-IT-Professional-Ethics.pdf.

Index

Page numbers followed by *f* refer to figures.

bot(s). *See also* chatbots
content development, 21–22
curation by, 23–24
for managing course registration/
payment, 24
robots vs., 17
smart vs. "dumb," 34–35
translation by, 22–23
as writers, 20–22
bot script, example of, 28*f*
brain, 12, 25, 35
and human behavior, 72–73
and learning management systems,
50–51
neuroplasticity of, 66
Brain Ladies, 11
branching, 36
broken links, identifying, 21
build vs. buy decision
with chatbots, 44–45
tool for, 95–96
business analytics, 52

C

Caballar, Rina Diane, 27
Carr, Nicholas, 49
Carroll, Lewis, 13
Castaway (film), 26
Centers for Disease Control and Prevention (CDC), 37
Chalmers, David, 4
chatbot(s), 31–46
brief history of, 38
and build vs. buy decision, 44–45
and coronavirus pandemic, 36–37
definition of, 34
examples of, 34, 36*f*
and natural language processing,
33–34
planner for, 100–101
popularity of, 38–40
potential opportunities provided by,
35–36
as relatively slow interface, 44
and smart vs. "dumb" bots, 34–35
24/7 performance coaching provided
by, 41–44
using, in education and training
programs, 40–44

China, 54, 78
Chollet, François, 5
coaching, interactive, 36
cobra effect, 74–75
cognition, augmented, 83
Cold War, x
Collins, Michael, x
Collins, Stella, 11
Common European Framework of Reference for Languages (CEFR), 60
computer program, first, 7
consciousness, 4
content development bots, 21–22
contextuality, 51
conversational interface, 62–63
conversational learning, 35
conversations, 38–39
Cope, David, 77
coronavirus pandemic (COVID-19
pandemic), ix–xii, 9, 24–25, 29, 36–37,
71, 72, 85–86
Correctional Offender Management
Profiling for Alternative Sanctions
(COMPAS), 75–76
Cortana, 20, 38
Cosmos (Sagan), 4
Coursera, 23, 48
course registration and payment,
management of, 24
COVID-19. *See* coronavirus pandemic
"creepiness" factor, 28
Csikszentmihalyi, Mihaly, 83
curation, 23–24, 43, 62
curriculum customization, 40
customer care, 60
customization, 60
cyberillusionism, 27

D

Dartmouth College, 8
data, structured vs. unstructured, 56
data analytics, 52–54, 55*f*
data mining, 52
Dawkins, Richard, 51
decision making, 7, 41
Deep Blue, 8
deep learning, 54, 55*f*
DeepMind, 9

Neuro-Link, 25
neuroplasticity, 66
neuroscience, xii–xiii, 12–13, 73
new employee onboarding bot, 41
new manager bot, 42
New York Times, 78
"next best decision" tests, 82
Nijsmans, Katelijn, 11

O

O'Connor, Trish, 27
one-page product guides, drafting, 21
organizational metrics, 21

P

PaintBot, 77
Parkinson's Law, 30
Pearson, 60
people skills, 25
performance support, providing, 63
personalized content, AI for, 10
pets, 26
pharmaceuticals, 73
Pike, Bob, 10
Pitts, Walter, 8
"plagiarism," AI, 77
planning, for learning management
    systems, 61
popular media, robots as depicted in,
    15–16
positive outcomes, focusing on, 82–83
pre-employment screenings, 65
presentation slides, populating, 21
presidential election of 2016, 8–9
Psychology Today, 52

R

reading, recommended, 103–104
Reagan, Ronald, 82
Rebooting AI (Marcus), 79
recommender systems, 52
recruiting process, learning management
    systems in, 63–65
reflect, challenges to, 40–41
Rembrandt van Rijn, 77
reports, running, 22
requests for proposals (RFPs), 45
retention, assessing, 43

reward cycle, 49–50
reward learning, 65
robotic instructors, 54
robot(s), 15–30
    bots vs., 17
    as employee replacement, 17–26
    first, 7–8
    in popular media, 15–16
rule-based automated systems, 53
rules, for AI, 79–84
Russia, 8–9

S

Sagan, Carl, 4
sales coach bot, 42
Samsung, 83
Schatsky, David, 6
self-driving cars, 16, 26
The Selfish Game (Dawkins), 51
Shane, Janelle, 75
Singhal, Shubham, 25
singularity, 6–7
Siri, 18, 20, 38, 63
    tips for training, 94
Skill Blueprints, 93
skimming, vi–vii
Skinner, B. F., 74
smart bots, 34–35
smart curation, 62
smart learning management systems,
    59–61
"smart reply" (Google), 33
Smyth, Annabelle, 61
Sneader, Kevin, 25
social learning, 52, 87
social media, vi, 8–9
Socratic method, 35
soft skills, 25
software as a service (SaaS), 45
Soviet Union, x
space race, x–xi
Sparko (robotic dog), 7
specialized AI, applications of, 5–6
sponsor regulation, 82
spreadsheets, 56, 57
Star Trek: Enterprise (TV show), 16
Sternberg, R. J., 4
Stewart, Potter, 6
storyboards, creating, 21

strange new world, AI as, 87
structured data, 56
"stuck" users, 40
styles, artistic, 77
subject matter experts (SMEs), 21
Sumser, John, 75
suppliers
    chatbot, 44–45
    tool for choosing, 97–98
    tool for managing, 99
support, providing, 63

T

Tay (chatbot), 66, 76
TD magazine, 57
Teachable, 48
television shows, robots as depicted in,
    15–16
Tesla, Nikola, 7
Theranos, 69
Through the Looking-Glass (Carroll), 13
Tilden, Mark, 79–80
Tipton, Shannon, 35
top performers, identifying, 21
translation, 22–23
transparency, of AI, 78–79
Turing, Alan, 8, 38, 61
Turing Test, 8
Twitter, 66
two-way conversations, 39

U

Udacity, 34
Uhl, Trish, 10
unknown unknowns, 79
unstructured data, 56
U.S. Army, 78
U.S. Department of Education, 43, 59
user attention, directing, 42–43
user interface
    for chatbots, 34
    conversational, 62–63

V

van Dinteren, Ria, 11
Van Gogh, Vincent, 77
variety (of data), 56
velocity (of data), 56

veracity (of data), 56–57
Vermeulen, André, 25
Vimeo, 23
virtual private networks (VPNs), 32
virtuous cycle, of data and AI, 58
Vivaldi, Antonio, 77
Volkswagen, 69
volume (of data), 55–56
von Neumann, John, 6–7

W

Washington Post, 20
Watson, 8
Waxter, Sandra, 80
weapons, 78
Wells Fargo Bank, 69
Westinghouse, 7
Westworld (TV show), 16
World Health Organization (WHO), 37
writers, robot, 20–22

Y

YouTube, 19, 23

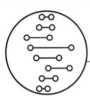

About the Author

Margie Meacham, "The Brain Lady," is a scholar-practitioner in the field of education and learning and president of LearningToGo. She specializes in practical applications for neuroscience to enhance learning and performance. Meacham's clients include businesses, schools, and universities. She writes a popular blog for ATD and has published the book *Brain Matters: How to Help Anyone Learn Anything Using Neuroscience.*

She first became interested in the brain when she lived with undiagnosed dyslexia as a child. Although she struggled in the early grades, she eventually taught herself how to overcome the challenge of a slight learning disability and became her high school valedictorian, graduated magna cum laude from Centenary University, and earned her master's degree in education from Capella University with a 4.0.

Meacham started her professional career in high-tech sales, and when she was promoted to director of training, she discovered her passion for teaching and helping people learn. She became one of the first corporate trainers to use video conferencing and e-learning and started her own consulting company from there. Today she consults for many organizations, helping them design learning experiences that will form new neural connections and marry neuroscience theory with practice.